PRAYING *with the* SAINTS

PRAYING *with the* SAINTS

MAKING THEIR PRAYERS YOUR OWN

WOODEENE KOENIG-BRICKER

LOYOLAPRESS.
CHICAGO

LOYOLAPRESS.

3441 N. ASHLAND AVENUE
CHICAGO, ILLINOIS 60657

Acknowledgments continued on p. 257.

Cover design by Claudia Smelser
Interior design by Tracey Harris

Library of Congress Cataloging-in-Publication Data
Koenig-Bricker, Woodeene.
Praying with the saints : making their prayers your own / Woodeene Koenig-Bricker.
p. cm.
ISBN 0-8294-1755-9
1. Prayers. 2. Christian saints—Biography. I. Title.

BV245 .K64 2001
242'.802—dc21

2001035835

Printed in Canada
01 02 03 04 05 Webcom 10 9 8 7 6 5 4 3 2 1

Introduction

I've collected prayers of the saints for years. I haven't a clue where I found most of them. Torn from church bulletins; copied from old novena, funeral, and Mass cards; jotted in notebooks; scribbled in my day planner—they have been part of my life for most of my life. I've sometimes shared a few with friends (I know of several non-Catholics who now use St. Julian of Norwich's prayer beginning "All shall be well" on a regular basis), but I gathered them primarily for my own edification and enjoyment. I am delighted to have been given the opportunity to share some of them with you.

There is a saying in theology: *Lex orandi, lex credendi.* Loosely translated, it means that what you say when you pray is what you believe. If that's so, then the prayers in this collection probably reflect as much of my own theology as they do of the saints who prayed them, for the major criterion for inclusion was simple: I had to like the prayer.

Because I generally prefer the plain to the flowery, the clear to the obscure, and the straightforward to the enigmatic, the prayers I like best tend to be plain, clear, and straightforward. But every now and again, I've been enchanted with a distinctive turn of phrase, such as St. John of the Cross's haunting line "If only I could die because then I would not die"; St. Augustine's exquisite "Too late I have loved you, O Beauty of ancient days, yet ever new"; or Thérèse of Lisieux's girlish cry to her patron, Joan of Arc. Therefore, I've included these prayers as well.

Unlike some collections of prayers that concentrate on very long poem-prayers and hundreds of authors, this compilation is, I hope, succinct and pithy. The fact is that most of my favorites are also short, sometimes very short—often no more than a few words. Some are brief because they were recorded on the saint's deathbed, and few people give lengthy speeches as they expire. But more often they are concise because our deepest and most heartfelt prayers tend to be brief. I think of Jesus' own words on the cross, "My God, my God, why have you forsaken me?"

I hope the brevity of these prayers is not off-putting, because the point of my own collection, from which they were drawn, was not to have reams of words to look at or to use as a reference, but rather to have prayers that could be easily memorized and carried in my heart. After all, it is only those words that are written on the pages of our hearts and minds that truly influence our lives.

Certainly the prayers contained here do not represent all the prayers of all the saints; they don't even represent all the prayers of the saints represented here. In fact, they may not even represent their best prayers. All saints went to Mass and joined in the great prayer that is the Eucharist. Many recited the traditional prayers of the church, such as the Liturgy of the Hours and the rosary. Many more used the psalms and Scripture as the basis for their dialogue with God.

Moreover, I wouldn't be the least surprised to learn that the greatest prayers came from saints who took seriously Christ's admonition to pray in their rooms in secret and thus never wrote their words down for posterity and never said them aloud when their followers could record them. We will never know those prayers until we hear them before the throne of God in heaven.

Having worked as a journalist for most of my adult life, I had one other bias in collecting these prayers. I wanted to be as certain as possible that the saint actually said or wrote the prayer or a close approximation of it. That's why you won't find here the famous prayer attributed to St. Francis that begins "Make me an instrument of your peace." It's a wonderful prayer, but Francis never said it. He lived its message, but the words themselves were penned by an Anglican clergyman who, it is believed, copied them onto the back of a holy card picturing St. Francis. And thus was born one of our most enduring modern myths!

I am often asked which prayer is my favorite. I have two actually. The first is Julian of Norwich's "All shall be well and all shall be well and all manner of thing shall be well." Her words never fail to bring me comfort and consolation. The second is Gregory of Nazianzus's prayer that begins "Alas, dear Christ, the Dragon is here again. Alas, he is here: terror has seized me, and fear." I have seen my fair share of dragons and I empathize completely with Gregory.

I hope you will find at least one or two prayers here that will resonate within your soul and accompany you forever on your journey of faith. If so, then I am doubly blessed—to be able to pray with the saints and to be able to share some of their prayers with you.

St. Agnes

third century

Stories about St. Agnes tend to be more fanciful than historic, but we do know she was a real person—one of the first saints of Christendom. Early writers St. Ambrose, Pope Damasus I, and Prudentius mention her. Even today her name is invoked in the Canon of the Mass (she's in the long list of names in Eucharistic Prayer I).

Accounts of her life generally agree that she was the beautiful daughter of Christian parents and had consecrated herself to perpetual virginity. Because of her vow, she refused the advances of a pagan suitor. Not only did she do that, but she compounded matters by publicly making the sign of the cross instead of worshiping a pagan god. This didn't sit well in Rome at the time of Emperor Diocletian, who wasn't fond of Christians on his best days. After being sent to a house of prostitution, Agnes was burned at the stake. (Or maybe beheaded. Or both. Stories of her life get a little confusing.) At any rate, Agnes is one of the famous martyrs of the early church, and her prayer is as relevant today as it was so many centuries ago.

When Death Is Near

I bless you, O Father, worthy as you are of highest praise, who renders me fearless even in the middle of the flames and who fills me with longing to go to you. Lo! I already behold Him whom I have trusted; I am about to grasp what I have hoped for; I embrace Him whom I have so ardently desired.

Blessed Alcuin of York

c. 730–804

Sometimes called "the schoolmaster of Europe," Blessed Alcuin was a friend and adviser of the emperor Charlemagne and was also deeply involved in the education of Charlemagne's sons, offering them sound advice on Christian living, among other things.

Although he probably wasn't a priest, or even a monk for that matter, he became the abbot of the monastery of St. Martin at Tours (something that could never happen today) and was responsible for liturgical reforms that have extended over the centuries. He revised the lectionary, assembled a new sacramentary, and wrote verse, textbooks, and a plethora of letters.

Despite having been written nearly fifteen hundred

years ago, his prayers reflect concerns as contemporary as today's headlines.

Prayer for When Questions Loom

Christ, why do you allow wars and massacres on earth? By what mysterious judgment do you allow innocent people to be cruelly slaughtered? I cannot know. I can only find assurance in the promise that your people will find peace in heaven, where no one makes war. As gold is purified by fire, so you purify souls by these bodily tribulations, making them ready to be received above the stars in your heavenly home.

Prayer for Mercy

Eternal Light, shine into our hearts;
Eternal Goodness, deliver us from evil;
Eternal Power, be our support;
Eternal Wisdom, scatter the darkness of our ignorance;
Eternal Pity, have mercy upon us—
So that with all our heart and mind and soul and strength
We may seek your face,
And be brought by your infinite mercy into your holy presence
Through Jesus Christ our Lord.

St. Alphonsus Liguori

1696–1787

St. Alphonsus Liguori, a hotshot lawyer in eighteenth-century Italy, abandoned the law when he lost an important case because of corruption in the courts. His disillusionment with the legal system set him on a new and more rewarding career path—the priesthood. After entering religious life, he worked as a preacher in Naples and eventually founded his own religious order, the Redemptorists.

Against his desire for anonymity, he was named bishop of Sant' Agata. There he worked tirelessly for his congregations despite being virtually crippled by arthritis.

Although he was a serious man, he had a lighter side as well. He loved attending the theater and listening to the music. In order to avoid scandal (theatrical productions in those days, as now, could tend to the risqué), he would buy a ticket for the back row and take off his glasses. Being extremely nearsighted, he could thus enjoy the tunes without being exposed to the tawdry show.

The erudition, logic, and keen use of language that served him in court are evident in his prayers, which also show his practical side.

Forgive the Past

O God of love, do you, then, so much desire to dispense your favors to us and yet are we so little anxious to obtain them? Oh, what sorrow will we feel at the hour of death, when we think of this negligence, so pernicious to our souls? O my Lord, forget, I beseech you, all that is past; for the future, with your help, I will prepare myself better by endeavoring to detach my affections from everything that prevents me from receiving all those graces which you desire to give me.

To the Holy Spirit

Holy Spirit, divine Consoler, I adore you as my
true God, with God the Father and God the Son.

I adore you and unite myself to the adoration you receive from the angels and saints.
I give you my heart and I offer my ardent thanksgiving for all the grace which you never cease to bestow on me.

For Five Graces

Eternal Father, your Son has promised that you would grant all the graces we ask of you in his name. Trusting in this promise, and in the name of and through the merits of Jesus Christ, I ask of you five special graces:

First, I ask pardon for all the offenses I have committed, for which I am sorry with all my heart, because I have offended your infinite goodness.

Second, I ask for your divine Light, which will enable me to see the vanity of all the things of this earth, and see also your infinite greatness and goodness.

Third, I ask for a share in your love, so that I can detach myself from all creatures, especially from myself, and love only your holy will.

Fourth, grant me the grace to have confidence in the merits of Jesus Christ and in the intercession of Mary.

Fifth, I ask for the grace of perseverance, knowing that whenever I call on you for assistance, you will answer my call and come to my aid;

I fear only that I will neglect to turn to you in time of need, and thus bring myself to ruin.

Grant me the grace to pray always, O Eternal Father, in the name of Jesus.

Morning Offering

My most sweet Lord, I offer and consecrate to you this morning all that I am and have:
My senses, my thoughts, my affections, my desires, my pleasures, my inclinations, my liberty.
In a word, I place my whole body and soul in your hands.

God's Goodness

O my God, you have treated us with so much love.
Help us to realize what a great Good you really are.
Never allow us to forget your goodness and love.

Short Prayers

Do you build up or tear down, O Lord, as seems good in your sight? I am content. I wish only what you wish.

Lord, I wish neither to be well nor to remain sick; I want only what you will.

May the divine will be loved and praised! May the Immaculate Virgin be also praised!

St. Angela Merici of Brescia

1474–1540

Founder of the oldest teaching order of women in the church, St. Angela placed her sisters under the care of St. Ursula, hence the name Ursulines.

Angela was a woman ahead of her time, seeking a lifestyle for women that allowed them to consecrate themselves to God but did not require them to enter convents. Instead, her sisters lived at home and "bloomed where they were planted."

Although she experienced many mystical visions, she was also a practical and capable organizer (the rules for her order have an almost military precision about them). Her prayers reflect her readiness to do God's will.

Prayers of Dedication to God

O my God, speak, your servant is listening and is ready to obey you in all things.

My Savior, illumine the darkness of my heart, and grant me grace rather to die than to offend your Divine Majesty any more. Guard, O Lord, my affections and my senses, that they may not stray, nor lead me away from the light of your face, the satisfaction of every afflicted heart.

I ask you, Lord, to receive all my self-will that by the infection of sin is unable to distinguish good from evil. Receive, O Lord, all my thoughts, words, and deeds, interior and exterior, that I lay at the feet of your Divine Majesty. Although I am utterly unworthy, I beseech you to accept all my being.

St. Anselm

c. 1033–1109

A theologian, scholar, and teacher, St. Anselm was often embroiled in bitter battles with English kings over the rights of the church. The situation got so bad that he was twice sent into exile for refusing to allow the king to invest bishops. Eventually he wrangled a compromise, in which kings were allowed some secular authority over bishops but were not permitted to usurp the spiritual authority that rightly belonged to the church.

Never one to shirk when a controversy was at hand, Anselm even got an ecclesiastical council to pass a resolution against slavery at a time when such a stance was almost unheard of.

A Doctor of the church, Anselm incorporated in his writing his reliance on reason to defend the faith. Faith seeking understanding was his life's motto. Perhaps because he was involved in so many bitter controversies, his prayers, like those of many other saints, beg God to be slow to anger and quick to forgive.

Prayer of a Dull Servant

My prayer is but a cold affair, Lord,
because my love burns with so small a flame,
but you who are rich in mercy
will not mete out to them your gifts
according to the dullness of my zeal,
but as your kindness is above all human love
so let your eagerness to hear
be greater than the feeling in my prayers.
Do this for them and with them, Lord,
so that they may speed according to your will
and thus ruled and protected by you,
always and everywhere,
may they come at last to glory and eternal rest,
through you who are living and reigning God,
through all ages.

For Understanding

O Lord,
you are my Lord and my God,

yet I have never seen you.
You have created and redeemed me,
and have conferred on me all my good,
yet I know you not.
I was created in order that I might know you,
but I have not yet attained the goal of my creation.
I confess, O Lord,
and give you thanks,
that you have created me in your image,
so that I might be mindful of you
and contemplate you and love you.
I seek not to understand in order that I may
believe;
rather, I believe in order that I may understand.

St. Anthony Mary Claret

1807–1870

One would think that someone who preached more than ten thousand sermons, published two hundred books and pamphlets on Christianity, and confirmed more than one hundred thousand people would have few, if any, doubts about his faith. Yet St. Anthony Mary Claret, founder of the Claretian Order and archbishop of Santiago de Cuba, Cuba, prayed not only for virtues such as goodness and chastity but also for the ability to believe and hope more completely in the teachings of Christ.

A man with a sense of destiny, he was not only a writer himself but the publisher of the Religious Library, which distributed five million books in twenty years. In his fifties he served as confessor to Spain's Queen Isabella II. At her court, he founded a laboratory and music and language schools, as well as a museum and a school. His followers, the Claretians, continue to spread the message of the gospel throughout the world.

His prayers reflect his practical approach to both faith and preaching the gospel.

For an Increase in Devotion

I believe, Lord, but let me believe more firmly.
I hope, Lord, but let me hope more surely.
I love, Lord, but let me love more warmly.
I repent, Lord, but let me repent more deeply.

Request for God's Gifts of Virtue

Father, give me humility, meekness, chastity, patience, and charity.
Father, teach me goodness, knowledge, and discipline.
Father, give me your love together with your grace and I will be rich enough.
My God, my Jesus, and my all.

A Writer's Prayer

O my God, I give you my word that I shall preach, write, and circulate good books and pamphlets in abundance, so as to drown evil in a flood of good.

St. Anthony of Padua

1195–1231

"Tony, Tony, turn around. Something's lost and must be found!"

For most Catholic Christians, St. Anthony of Padua is *the* saint to turn to when something has been lost and must be found. The son of Portuguese nobility ("of Padua" refers to the Italian city where he did much of his ministry), St. Anthony first joined the Augustinians, but when the relics of some Franciscan martyrs were brought through his town, he was so inspired by the story of their lives that he decided to enter their order.

How did this preacher and teacher become the patron saint of lost car keys and lost wallets? No one is sure how the custom developed, but one anecdote centers on a friar who stole a valuable book from Anthony. Anthony is said to have prayed for its return, and for whatever reason—take your pick: supernatural intervention, guilty conscience, mystical vision—the friar brought back the manuscript. Hence, Anthony has been permanently assigned to the heavenly lost and found department.

For Love of Neighbor

Lord Jesus, bind us to you and to our neighbor with love. May our hearts not be turned away from you. May our souls not be deceived nor our talents or minds enticed by allurements of error, so that we may never distance ourselves from your love. Thus may we love our neighbor as ourselves with strength, wisdom, and gentleness. With your help, you who are blessed throughout all ages.

The Victorious Cross

Behold the Cross of the Lord!
Begone you enemy powers!
The Lion of the Tribe of Judah,
The Root of David, has conquered.
Alleluia!

ST. AUGUSTINE

354–430

St. Augustine's most famous prayer is probably his shortest: "Lord, make me chaste, but not yet." Augustine had good reason to dawdle in asking for chastity—he lived openly with his mistress for many years and fathered a son with her. Needless to say, his lifestyle gave his saintly mother, Monica, her share of gray hairs.

Augustine was raised to be a Christian but, according to the custom of his time, put off baptism while taking up other pursuits. His more reputable activities included studying philosophy and opening a school of rhetoric.

His conversion is one of the most remarkable in history. At age thirty-two, he opened the Bible at random and read the first lines he saw, from Paul's letter to the Romans: "Not in orgies and drunkenness, not in promiscuity and licentiousness, not in rivalry and jealousy. But put on the Lord Jesus Christ and make no provision for the desires of the flesh."

Following his baptism by St. Ambrose, he became one of the great champions of the church—and finally made his mother proud.

His prayers are among the most beautiful and passionate ever written.

Too Late I Have Loved You

Too late I have loved you, O Beauty of ancient days, yet ever new? Too late I have loved you! And behold, you were within, and I abroad, and there I searched for you; I was deformed, plunging amid those fair forms, which you had made. You were with me, but I was not with you. Things held me far from you—things which, if they were not in you, were not at all. You called, and shouted, and burst my deafness. You flashed and shone, and scattered my blindness. You breathed odors and I drew in breath—and I pant for you. I tasted, and I hunger and I thirst. You touched me, and I burned for your peace.

Master of Nature

O God, by whose laws the poles revolve, the stars follow their courses, the sun rules the day, and the moon presides over the night; and all the world maintains, as far as this world of sense allows, the wondrous stability of things by means of the orders and recurrences of seasons: through the days by the changing of light and darkness, through the months by the moon's progressions and declines, through the years by the successions of Spring, Summer, Autumn, and Winter, through the cycles by the completion of the sun's course, through the great eras of time by the return of the stars to their starting points.

For Light in Dark Times

God of life, there are days when the burdens we carry chafe our shoulders and wear us down; when the road seems dreary and endless, the skies gray and threatening; when our lives have no music in them and our hearts are lonely, and our souls have lost their courage. Flood the path with light, we beseech you; turn our eyes to where the skies are full of promise.

Restless Hearts

Our hearts are restless, O Lord, until they rest in you.

St. Basil the Great

329–379

It's one of history's little jokes that a saint with "great" in his name sounds like an ordinary kitchen spice. Perhaps it is fitting, since Basil was definitely a spicy saint—an indefatigable opponent of heresy and a tireless advocate for the truth. Perhaps his passion stemmed from being surrounded by saints; his best friend was St. Gregory of Nazianzus and his sister was St. Macrina. (Talk about friends in high places!) He also was a staunch defender of the separation of church and state, insisting that government has no place in regulating religion. A man of deep conviction, he took no guff from anyone, including the emperor Valens.

As a young man, Basil considered joining a monastery, but he wasn't impressed with any he visited, so he established his own on his family's estate. His rule, or set of laws, for his monks helped shape monastic life in the East. One of his rule's major tenets was an emphasis on activity, especially serving others, not just spending time in contemplation or mental prayer. He himself worked in a soup kitchen, tended ladies of ill repute, and nursed the sick.

Prayer for Guidance

O Lord, we beseech you, to ask for the gift we need. Steer the ship of our life to yourself, the quiet harbor of all storm-stressed souls. Show us the course which we are to take. Renew in us the spirit of docility. Let your Spirit curb our fickleness; guide and strengthen us to perform what is for our own good, to keep your commandments, and ever to rejoice in your glorious and vivifying presence. Yours is the glory and praise for all eternity. Amen.

St. Benedict of Nursia

c. 480–547

Ironically, the man who is often called the Father of Western Monasticism set out to be a hermit. In his twenties, he tried to escape the glory, splendor, and debauchery of Rome by hiding out in a cave and subjecting his mind and body to rigorous prayer and fasting. It was a good plan, but unfortunately it didn't work. Attracted by his reputation for holiness, people began hanging around his cave. What was he to do but organize them into communities? Thus began the development of the first monasteries in Europe.

Benedict might have been just another holy founder except for one thing: the rule, or canon for life, that he set down for his monks has continued to be used even today in many modern monasteries. He was as influential in shaping Western monasticism as

St. Basil was in shaping the Eastern. Placing equal emphasis on prayer, work, and study, Benedict's Rule is a model of the Christian way of life. His prayers, like his rule, reflect his practical nature.

Benedict's Pledge

O Lord,
I place myself in your hands and dedicate myself to you.
I pledge myself to do your will in all things—
To love the Lord God with all my heart, all my soul, all my strength.
Not to kill, not to steal, not to covet, not to bear false witness,
to honor all persons.
Not to do to another what I should not want done to myself.
To chastise the body.
Not to seek after pleasures. To love fasting. To relieve the poor.
To clothe the naked. To visit the sick. To bury the dead.
To help in trouble. To console the sorrowing.
To hold myself aloof from worldly ways.
To prefer nothing to the love of Christ.
Not to give way to anger.

Not to foster a desire for revenge.
Not to entertain deceit in the heart.
Not to make a false peace. Not to forsake charity.
Not to swear, lest I swear falsely.
To speak the truth with heart and tongue.
Not to return evil for evil.
To do no injury, indeed, even to bear patiently any
injury done to me.
To love my enemies.
Not to curse those who curse me
but rather to bless them.
To bear persecution for justice' sake.
Not to be proud.
Not to be given to intoxicating drink.
Not to be an overeater.
Not to be lazy.
Not to be slothful.
Not to be a murmurer.
Not to be a detractor.
To put my trust in God.
To refer the good I see in myself to God.
To refer any evil I see in myself to myself.
To fear the day of judgement.
To be in dread of hell.
To desire eternal life with spiritual longing.
To keep death before my eyes daily.
To keep constant watch over my actions.
To remember that God sees me everywhere.

To call upon Christ for defense against evil thoughts that arise in my heart.
To guard my tongue against wicked speech.
To avoid much speaking.
To avoid idle talk.
Not to seek to appear clever.
To read only what is good to read.
To pray often.
To ask forgiveness daily for my sins, and to seek ways to amend my life.
To obey my superiors in all things rightful.
Not to desire to be thought holy, but to seek holiness.
To fulfill the commandments of God by good works.
To love chastity.
To hate no one.
Not to be jealous or envious of anyone.
Not to love strife.
Not to love pride.
To honor the aged.
To pray for my enemies.
To make peace after a quarrel, before the setting of the sun.
Never to despair of your mercy, O God of Mercy.

Desire of a Devout Believer

Grant, O Gracious,
O Holy Father,
Upon me to bestow:
Intellect to understand you,
Perceptions to perceive you,
Reason to discern you,
Diligence to seek you,
Wisdom to find you,
A spirit to know you.

St. Bernadette Soubirous

1844–1879

If there were such a thing as a saint-selecting bookie, Bernadette probably wouldn't have been on anyone's shortlist. Nothing about her suggested sainthood. She was sickly, uneducated, poor, and not especially bright. She wasn't even particularly pious: at age fourteen she still hadn't made her first communion. Talk about a dark horse in the saint race!

It's no wonder people were more than a little suspicious when this obscure French peasant girl reported having seen visions of a lady in white who called herself the Immaculate Conception. When the lady told her to scrabble in the earth and uncover a spring, little did Bernadette know that the trickle of water would become one of the most beloved sites of pilgrimage in the modern world.

Thousands travel to Lourdes each year to take the water and pray for a miracle.

Bernadette herself suffered greatly because of her association with Lourdes. She was hounded by the curious, investigated by authorities, and questioned by the skeptical. It's no wonder she had nothing to do with the development of the site; in fact, she didn't even attend the dedication of the basilica that was built there.

Prayer for a Changed Spirit

My God, when I pause and reflect upon my numberless shortcomings and your justice, I am appalled: fear paralyzes me. My God! Have mercy upon my misery and frailty. Let suffering and trial be my lot. They alone can destroy the old in me. Divine life is only possible in making the sacrifice of human nature. There is no alternative; I must make this sacrifice if I desire to save my soul.

Bread of Life

O Jesus, give me, I pray, the Bread of humility, the Bread of obedience, the Bread of charity, the Bread of patience to bear the sufferings of my poor heart. O Jesus, you want me to be crucified, fiat! Give me the Bread of strength to suffer as I ought, the Bread of seeing only you in all things and all ways. Jesus, Mary, the Cross: I want no other friends but these.

Prayers from the Heart

O my Lord! If I may not shed my blood, and may not give my life for you, let me at least, O Lord, die to all that is displeasing to you.

O Jesus, I implore you: give to me the Bread of patience, and support the grief that tortures my heart.

O Jesus! Make me realize more fully the jealousy of divine love! Detach my affections from the mundane, raise them up, and bind them to yourself.

St. Bernard of Clairvaux

1090–1153

Even his friends said that St. Bernard of Clairvaux was sometimes "willful and hard," but he reserved his harshest discipline for himself. His stern ascetic nature caused him serious health problems, but his mystical nature and devotional writings have influenced thousands.

When he decided to enter the Benedictine monastery at Cîteaux, he convinced thirty-one friends, including some of his own brothers, to join with him. The story of their remarkable entrance into monastic life has been a source of inspiration over the centuries, but since at least a few of the men were married, one wonders what their wives thought of their action. It's possible that some of these wives were less kindly disposed to Bernardis, since their husbands' joining a religious order pretty much forced them into convents. On the other hand, if the marriages weren't all that happy, perhaps Bernard became one of their heroes!

This wasn't the only time Bernard got himself into controversy because of his zeal for the Lord. He preached the Second Crusade, which was a resounding failure, and consequently claimed that the crusade itself was divinely inspired, but the sins of the soldiers had brought it to ruin (which only goes to show that even a great saint isn't above a little blame shifting!).

His prayers reflect his utter confidence in Christ for strength and guidance.

The Heart of Jesus

Oh, how good and pleasant a thing it is to dwell in the Heart of Jesus!
Who is there that does not love a heart so wounded?
Who can refuse a return of love to a heart so loving?

Spiritual Struggle

Come Lord Jesus,
take away scandals from your kingdom which is my soul,
and reign there.
You alone have the right.
For greediness comes to claim a throne within me;
haughtiness and self-assertion would rule over me;
pride would be my king;
luxury says, "I will reign";
ambition, detraction, envy, and anger struggle within me for the mastery.
I resist as far as I am able;
I struggle according as help is given me.
I call on my Lord Jesus.
For his sake I defend myself,
since I acknowledge myself as wholly his possession.
He is my God,
Him I proclaim my Lord.
I have no other king than my Lord, Jesus Christ.
Come, then, O Lord, and disperse these enemies by your power,
and you shall reign in me, for you are my King and my God.

The Memorare

Remember, O most gracious Virgin Mary,
That never was it known

That anyone who fled to your protection,
Implored your help,
Or sought your intercession
Was left unaided.
Inspired by this confidence,
I fly to you,
O Virgin of Virgins, my mother,
To you I come;
Before you I stand sinful and sorrowful,
O Mother of the Word Incarnate.
Despise not my petitions
But in your mercy, hear and answer me. Amen.

St. Bonaventure

1217–1274

Settling a family squabble has to be one of the most thankless jobs in the world. St. Bonaventure had to deal with a terrible one—a massive dispute within the ranks of the Franciscans. Named minister general of the Friars Minor at age forty, he was immediately tossed into the throes of controversy. The order was split between those who wanted inflexible adherence to the old rules coupled with a severe and rigorous way of life and those who thought mitigation of the rule was necessary for continued expansion. Amazingly, Bonaventure was able to keep the order from imploding over such divergent points of view. Because of his ability to keep the order intact, he is sometimes called the second founder of the Franciscans.

His ability to reconcile divided factions was evident again near the end of his life when he helped the pope effect a reunion with the Greek church. At the first joint Mass on the feast day of Saints Peter and Paul (a fitting time, since Peter and Paul had their own issues to resolve), St. Bonaventure had the privilege of preaching the homily.

Hunger for the Lord

Pierce, O most sweet Lord Jesus, my inmost soul with the most joyous and healthful wound of your love, with true, serene, and most holy apostolic charity, that my soul may ever languish and melt with love and longing for you, that it may yearn for you and faint for your courts, and long to be dissolved and to be with you.

Grant that my soul may hunger after you, the bread of angels, the refreshment of holy souls and daily and supersubstantial bread, having all sweetness and savor and every delight of taste; let my heart ever hunger after and feed upon you, upon whom the angels desire to look, and may my inmost soul be filled with the sweetness of your savor; may it thirst after you, the fountain of life, the fountain of wisdom and knowledge, the fountain of eternal light, the torrent of pleasure, the richness of the house of God; may it ever compass you, seek you, find you, run to you, attain you, meditate upon you, speak of you, and do all things to the praise and glory of your name, with humility and discretion, with love and delight, with ease and affection, and with perseverance unto the end; may you alone be ever my hope, my entire assurance, my riches, my delight, my pleasure, my joy, my rest and tranquility, my peace, my sweetness, my fragrance, my sweet savor, my food, my refreshment, my refuge, my help, my wisdom, my portion, my possession, and my treasure, in whom may my mind and my heart be fixed and firm and root immovably henceforth and forever. Amen.

Short Prayer for Guidance

Lead me forth, Lord, in your way, and let me step in your truth; let my heart be glad, that it fears your Name.

St. Brigid of Ireland

c. 452–524

One of the most beloved Irish saints, Brigid's exploits are the stuff of legend. The real details of her life are lost in the byways of time, but that hasn't discouraged her devoted followers. Supposedly the daughter of a slave mother and a noble father, she is said to have built the first convent in Ireland, at Kildare. It wasn't quite like our convents, however, because it also contained a separate section for men.

Hospitality and generosity marked Brigid's life. The many legendary stories told about the saint include one that says she routinely gave the poor all the cream and butter from her cow, leaving the skim milk for the priests and bishops!

Her most famous prayer, with its opening line asking for a lake of ale, shows her down-to-earth good nature. Don't worry that a prayer asking for beer in lake-sized quantities might set a bad example. Irish ale in the sixth century wasn't nearly as strong as today's brews and was drunk by people of all ages.

Abundant Blessings

I should like a great lake of ale for the King of kings.
I should like the family of heaven to drink it through time eternal.
I would like the angels of heaven to be among us.
I would like an abundance of peace.
I would like full vessels of charity.
I would like rich treasures of mercy.
I would like cheerfulness to preside over all.
I would like Jesus to be present.
I would like the three Marys of illustrious renown to be with us.
I would like the friends of heaven to be gathered around us from all parts.
I would like myself to be a rent payer to the Lord; that I should suffer distress, that he would bestow a good blessing upon me.

Blessed Brother André

1845–1937

During the fifty years he spent as a brother in the Congregation of the Holy Cross, Blessed Brother André worked innumerable miracles on behalf of the sick and dying. Sometimes called the Miracle Worker of Montreal, he always attributed his many cures not to his own prayers but to the intercession of St. Joseph.

Brother André was not your stereotypical meek and mild saint. Although he had a good sense of humor and was considered a bit of a storyteller, he could be quite short-tempered, especially when he was tired. A story is told of a woman who came to him seeking a cure for lameness. He spoke so sharply to her that she left in tears, and it wasn't until some minutes later that she realized she had been cured. When he realized what he had done, he was filled with remorse and said, "At least they see that I am but a poor sinner."

PRAYERS FOR BUSY (AND SHORT-TEMPERED) PEOPLE

O Holy Angels, grant that I may be filled with the presence of God on the altar as you are penetrated by it in Heaven.

Here is the grain! *(His final words of prayer)*

Brother Lawrence

c. 1605–1691

Little is known about Nicholas Herman except that he was a soldier and hermit before entering a Carmelite monastery in Paris under the name Brother Lawrence. Although he spent most of his religious life as a kitchen worker, his world-famous guide to the spiritual life, *The Practice of the Presence of God,* shows his profound interior prayer life (and reveals a bit of the struggles that make him so beloved).

In God's Presence

O my God, since you art with me, and I must now, in obedience to your commands, apply my mind to these outward things, I beg you to grant me the grace to continue in your Presence; and to this end do you prosper me with your assistance, receive all my works, and possess all my affections.

Prayer of an Honest Heart

Lord, I cannot do this unless you enable me.

St. Caedmon

d.c. 680

Often what we know about one saint comes from the writings of another. Such is the case with St. Caedmon. The little we know about him comes from the writings of the Venerable Bede.

Bede relates that Caedmon, an elderly herdsman who lived near the Abbey of Whitby, would leave a party when it was his time to entertain the guests with a song, as was customary. (Talk about singing for your supper!) Once, having left early to avoid the entire situation, he had a dream in which someone—an angel, perhaps—appeared and told him to sing. After offering the usual "I can't do that" excuses, Caedmon sang a hymn of his own creation.

When Caedmon told St. Hilda about his dream, she promptly had him made a monk and set him to work writing spiritual poetry. Unfortunately, the only example of his writing is the following song of praise preserved by Bede.

Caedmon's Song: Praise to the Creator

Now must we praise the guardian of heaven,
the power and conception of the Lord, and all his works.
For he, eternal Lord, first created heaven as a roof;
he, the holy Maker for the sons of men.
Then the eternal keeper of mankind
furnished the earth below,
the land for men, almighty God and everlasting Lord.

St. Catherine dei Ricci

1522–1590

For twelve years St. Catherine dei Ricci, an Italian visionary, relived the passion of Christ each week from noon on Thursday until 4:00 P.M. on Friday. Although unconscious, she reenacted all the events, including the scourging, the crowning with thorns, and the nailing to the cross. She was also one of the first saints to bear the mystical marks of Christ's wounds, the stigmata, on her own body. (St. Francis of Assisi is the first known stigmatist.)

Despite the fact that she is one of the great mystics of the church, she was also a very practical woman. She disliked her stigmata and the reliving of the Passion, calling them an inconvenience and an embarrassment. She prayed that God take back his unwanted gift. God did.

For many years she ran a Dominican convent, where she was known for her practical advice and faithful teaching of the truth. Each Friday shortly before retiring, she said the following prayer, which consists of verses from the psalms and the Gospels interwoven into a deeply moving meditation on the Passion.

In Remembrance of the Passion

My friends and my neighbors
Have drawn near and stood against me.
(Ps 38 [37]:12)
I was delivered up, and came not forth:
my eyes languished through poverty.
(Ps 88 [87]:9–10)
And his sweat came down as drops of blood,
trickling on the ground. (Lk 22:44)
For many dogs have encompassed me,
the council of the malignant has besieged me.
(Ps 22 [21]:17)
I have given my body to the strikers
and my cheeks to them that plucked them.
(Is 50:6a)
I have not turned my face from them that
rebuked me,
and spit upon me. (Is 50:6b)

For I am ready for scourges,
and my sorrow is continually before me.
(Ps 39 [38]:18)
And pleating a crown of thorns,
they put it on his head. (Mt 27:29)
They have pierced my hands and my feet;
they have numbered all my bones. (Ps 22 [21]:18)
And they gave me gall for my food,
and in my thirst they gave me vinegar to drink.
(Ps 69 [68]:22)
All they that saw me have laughed me to scorn;
they have spoken with the lips and wagged the head. (Ps 22 [21]:8)
They have looked and stared upon me.
They have parted my garments amongst them;
and upon my vesture they have cast lots.
(Ps 22 [21]:18b–19)
Into your hands I commend my spirit:
you have redeemed me, O Lord, the God of truth.
(Ps 31 [30]:6)
Look, we beg you, O Lord, upon this your household for whom
Our Lord Jesus Christ did not hesitate to give himself over into
the hands of sinners and undergo the torment of the Cross.

St. Catherine of Genoa

1447–1510

Being a mystic is difficult under ordinary circumstances; being a mystic married to an unfaithful spendthrift with a nasty temper would seem to be almost impossible. Yet St. Catherine of Genoa did it.

It wasn't easy. The difficulties in her life caused her to fall into a deep depression, and it was only by the grace of God and the apparent intercession of St. Benedict that she recovered.

Ultimately her devotion (and a fortuitous bankruptcy) converted her husband, Julian, and together they worked for twenty years serving the poor and sick. Eventually they moved into a hospital where Catherine acted as the manager, dealing with a devastating outbreak of the plague, among other things. After Julian's death she cared for his illegitimate daughter, even remembering her in her will.

A Holy Exchange

Lord, I make you a present of myself.
I do not know what to do with myself.
Let me, then, Lord, make this exchange:
I will place this evil being into your hands.
You are the only one who can hide it in your
  goodness and can so rule over me
That nothing will be seen of my own proper self.
On your part, you will grant your pure love,
Which will extinguish all other loves in me
And will annihilate me and busy me so much with
  you
That I will have no time or place for anything or
  anyone else.

O tender Love, I want all of you. I could not live if I thought I were to do without even a spark of you.

St. Catherine of Siena

1347–1380

Catherine of Siena, one of the church's greatest saints, was remarkably brave, so courageous, in fact, that she upbraided the pope for his shortcomings. When the pope was in exile in Avignon, Catherine persuaded him to return to Rome. Later, when the papacy was divided between two men, she destroyed her health with prayers and petitions for the restoration of God's will.

Catherine was the youngest of twenty-five children (her mother was either a saint or totally exhausted—or both!). Although she is sometimes portrayed as a nun, she was actually a Third Order Dominican—a laywoman following a religious rule of life. When she wasn't traveling to see the pope or other notables of the era, she lived at home in Siena and gathered a group of like-minded disciples to help her serve the poor, the imprisoned, and the sick. Although she never had any children of her own, she must have been one of the original Earth Mothers, because her followers called her "Mama" due to her nurturing nature.

Catherine is one of only two women named a Doctor of the church. (Teresa of Ávila is the other one.) Her *Dialogue* is one of the great mystical treasures of the Middle Ages.

Mystical Fire

O abyss, O eternal Godhead, O sea profound, what more could you give me than yourself? You are the first that ever burns without being consumed; you consume in your heat all the soul's self-love; you are the fire which takes away cold; with your light you illuminate me so that I may know all your truth. Clothe me, clothe me with your eternal truth, so that I may run this mortal life with true obedience and with the light of your most holy faith.

Thanksgiving

O tender Father, you gave me more, much more than I ever thought to ask for. I realize that our human desires can never really match what you long to give us. Thanks and again thanks, O Father, for having granted my petitions, and that which I never realized I needed or petitioned.

The Sea of the Trinity

You, O eternal Trinity, are a deep sea, into which the more I enter the more I find, and the more I find the more I seek. The soul cannot be satiated in your abyss, for she continually hungers after you, the eternal Trinity, desiring to see you with the light of your light. As the hart desires the springs of living water, so my soul desires to leave the prison of this body and see you in truth.

Hymn to the Precious Blood

Precious Blood, Ocean of Divine Mercy: Flow upon us!
Precious Blood, most pure Offering: Procure for us every Grace!
Precious Blood, Hope and Refuge of sinners: Atone for us!
Precious Blood, Delight of holy souls: Draw us! Amen.

Venerable Charles de Foucauld

1858–1916

Charles de Foucauld, better known as Little Brother Charles of Jesus, spent the first part of his life living fast and free. He once said of a string of lovers, "I rent by the day, not the month." Charles did not have a sudden conversion; through the example and encouragement of his cousin, he slowly returned to the faith he had abandoned at age fifteen.

Following his recommitment to the Catholic Church, he tried living for nearly ten years in Trappist communities but felt unfulfilled in the monastic life. Seeking to emulate the "hidden life" of Jesus, he moved from his native France to Nazareth and lived as a hermit.

Finally ordained when he was forty-three, he moved again, this time to Algeria, where he had fought as a soldier. There in the desert, Venerable Charles came to understand that the mastery of self that he sought for holiness was not possible without the help of God. His gentle spirit and loving example garnered him many friends among his neighbors, although he was later murdered by a Muslim sect.

Prayer of Abandonment

Father, I abandon myself into your hands;
do with me what you will.
Whatever you may do, I thank you;
I am ready for all, I accept all.
Let only your will be done in me,
and in all your creatures—
I wish no more than this, O Lord.
Into your hands I commend my soul;
I offer it to you with all the love of my heart,
for I love you, Lord!
And so need to give myself,
surrender myself into your hands,
without reserve,
and with boundless confidence,
for you are my Father.

St. Charles Lwanga

d. 1886

The irony of using the words of the saints as prayers is that sometimes the greatest saints write down few if any of their prayers. In those cases, their lives themselves become their prayer. Thus it is with two of the greatest saints of African descent—Charles Lwanga of Uganda and Ven. Pierre Toussaint. (See page 193.)

Charles Lwanga's story begins with another Ugandan martyr, Joseph Mukasa. Mukasa was the captain of King Mwanga's pages. When he refused to participate in the king's drunken homosexual orgies and then compounded his situation by criticizing the murder of a Protestant missionary, the dissolute king had him beheaded. Lwanga succeeded Mukasa as captain of the pages. Because Lwanga also denied Mwanga access to the young men in his charge, the king went berserk and commanded a pogrom of all Christians in Uganda. Lwanga was one of the first to die, being slowly roasted over a fire. His final words are his only recorded prayer.

Prayer at the Moment of Death

Katonda wange!

"My God!"

St. Clare

1193–1253

From the first moment she heard St. Francis speak, St. Clare of Assisi was determined to follow his way of life. She snuck away from her friends and family, met Francis and his monks in secret, cut her hair, and put on the habit of the Franciscans. Although her family even used physical force to try to make her return home, she persisted in her resolve and finally won their support. In fact, her mother and sister eventually joined her. They lived according to Francis's rule of "Lady Poverty"—begging for their food and drink. She spent the rest of her life in a house near the Church of San Damiano, down the hillside from the city of her birth.

Clare is said to have been able to view the funeral of her mentor, St. Francis, even though she was miles away at the time. For this she was named the patroness of television.

Her prayers, like those of Francis, are filled with joy at the goodness of the Lord.

Hymn of Praise

Praise and glory to you, O loving Jesus Christ,
for the most sacred wound in your side,
and by that adorable wound and by your infinite mercy
which you made known to us in the opening of your breast to the soldier Longinus,
and so to us all.
I pray you, O most gentle Jesus,
having redeemed me by baptism from original sin,
so now, by your Precious Blood, which is offered and received throughout the world,
deliver me from all evils, past, present, and to come.
And by your most bitter death,
give me a lively faith, a firm hope, and a perfect charity,
so that I may love you with all my heart, all my soul, and all my strength;

make me firm and steadfast in good works and
grant me perseverance in your service
so that I may be able to please you always.

Peace

Go forth in peace, for you have followed the good road. Go forth without fear, for he who created you has made you holy, has always protected you, and loves you as a mother. Blessed be you, my God, for having created me.

St. Clement of Rome

d.c. 99

St. Clement was the third pope of the Catholic Church and the author of the First Epistle of Clement, one of the most important writings of the early church. Virtually everything else we know about him—such as his work with St. Paul or his martyrdom in the Crimea—is probably pious legend.

However, not far from the Colosseum in Rome stands the Church of San Clemente, where his relics are buried. Visitors to the church can wend their way down through the centuries under the basilica until they eventually arrive at a first-century temple to the Roman cult god Mithra. Far above the ancient altar, built for sacrificing bulls, St. Clement rests in solemn peace awaiting the Second Coming.

For the Poor and Lowly

We beseech you, O Lord, to grant us your help and protection.

Deliver the afflicted, pity the lowly, raise the fallen, reveal yourself to the needy, heal the sick, and bring home your wandering people. Feed the hungry, ransom the captive, support the weak, comfort the fainthearted. Let all the nations of the earth know that you alone are God, that Jesus Christ is our child, and that we are your people and the sheep of your pasture.

St. Clotilda

d.c. 545

What greater loss can a parent suffer than the death of a child? St. Clotilda's prayer at the death of her firstborn son encompasses both her faith and her anguish. Nevertheless, her sorrows were only beginning. Her other sons grew up to become continually embroiled in war and fratricide. It was only through her earnest prayers at the shrine of St. Martin that her last two sons did not kill each other in battle.

Her life was not all sorrow, however. Married to the Frankish king Clovis, Clotilda was apparently well loved by her somewhat brutish husband. Although he wasn't keen on having their children baptized (his enthusiasm for his wife's faith waned when their first son died on the day of his baptism), he let Clotilda have her way.

Eventually she saw her husband converted to Christianity, and with him, three thousand warriors and their families. Through her prayer and example, and with the effort of St. Remi, Clotilda brought the faith to the barbarian tribes of Europe.

At the Death of Her Son

I give thanks to Almighty God that He has not considered me unworthy to be the mother of a child admitted into the celestial kingdom. Having quitted the world in the white robe of his innocence, he will rejoice in the presence of God through all eternity.

St. Columba of Iona

c. 521–597

St. Columba, one of the most beloved Scottish saints, was actually Irish. A scholar by nature, he was inordinately fond of books and even got into a lawsuit with St. Finnian over a copy of St. Jerome's Psalter. King Diarmaid of Ireland ruled in favor of Finnian, something Columba didn't take kindly. When one of King Diarmaid's men killed someone under Columba's care, all hell broke loose. Columba went to war against the king, not only winning the battle and killing thousands but also recovering his Psalter in the process. (So much for forgive and forget.)

If the story ended there, Columba would hardly be a saint. But the story goes on. Columba was so repentant over the deaths his action caused that he exiled himself to the island of Iona off the Scottish coast, where he established a center of learning and culture. Because he never returned to Ireland, we can't be sure whether his exile was the result of self-discipline or self-preservation (the king's followers may have had long memories). Because of his intimate association with the Scots, he has become inexorably identified with that country.

While gentleness was never one of his virtues, he is said to have mellowed in his old age, praying simply that he be allowed to "keep a door in paradise."

Doorkeeper in Heaven

Almighty Father, Son, and Holy Ghost, eternal ever-blessed gracious God; to me the least of saints, to me allow that I may keep a door in paradise. That I may keep even the smallest door, the furthest, the darkest, coldest door, the door that is least used, the stiffest door. If so it be but in your house, O God, if it so be that I can see your glory even afar, and hear your voice, O God, and know that I am with you, O God.

St. Dimitrii of Rostov

seventeenth century

Very little is known about St. Dimitrii, especially in the West, but his prayer is one of the classics of devotion in the Eastern Church.

Come, My Light

Come, my Light, and illumine my darkness.
Come, my Life, and revive me from death.
Come, my Physician, and heal my wounds.
Come, Flame of divine love, and burn up the thorns of my sins, kindling my heart with the flame of your love.
Come, my King, sit upon the throne of my heart and reign there.
For you alone are my King and my Lord.

St. Dominic

1170–1221

The founder of the Order of Preachers (Dominicans), St. Dominic has never received the same level of secular fame as his contemporary, St. Francis of Assisi. Yet Dominic's order has produced some of the greatest saints in the history of Christianity, including Catherine of Siena, Albert the Great, Thomas Aquinas, Rose of Lima, and Martin de Porres, to mention but a few.

Dominic was the well-loved youngest child of the Guzman family. When his mother was pregnant with him, she had a prophetic vision of a dog carrying a torch in its mouth, which she took as a sign that her child would bear the light of the Gospels to the entire world. Considering the prophecy, it is ironic that the word *Dominicans* and the Latin words *Domine Canes*, or "Hounds of God," look so much alike.

Dominic encouraged his followers to pray not just with words but with their entire bodies, hearts, and minds. His nine ways of prayer remain a model for all who desire to enter into complete union with God.

In this prayer, St. Dominic emphasizes the importance of preaching the gospel to all, something his thousands of priests, brothers, sisters, and lay members do to this day.

To Share the Gospel

May God the Father who made us bless us.
May God the Son send his healing among us.
May God the Holy Spirit move within us and give us
eyes to see with, ears to hear with, and hands that your work might be done.
May we walk and preach the word of God to all.
May the angel of peace watch over us and lead us at last
by God's grace to the Kingdom.

St. Edith Stein

1891–1942

Raised a devout Jew in Breslau, Germany (now Wroclaw, Poland), St. Edith Stein renounced her faith at age thirteen and became an atheist. A dedicated seeker of the truth, she was a professor of philosophy when she converted to Catholicism after reading Teresa of Ávila's autobiography.

Edith's conversion occurred not long before one of the century's great turning points—the rise of Adolph Hitler and his determination to eliminate all Jews from the face of the earth. Hitler's hatred left Edith in a paradoxical position: she was Catholic, but also Jewish. To the Nazis, her Jewishness mattered more. The Nazis had her fired from her teaching position because of her heritage.

After being forced out of the university, Edith

decided to fulfill a long-held desire to join the Carmelites at Cologne. As the Nazis began their execution of Jews, she moved to the Netherlands, but she was unable to escape the long arm of persecution. She and her sister who had also converted to Catholicism and who was with her at the time were arrested, removed from the Dutch convent where they were hiding, and transported to Auschwitz. She was executed there on August 9, 1942.

One of the most brilliant scholars of her time, Edith Stein was a woman of humility, compassion, and erudition. Her writings are filled with brilliant discourses on the faith, but as her prayers reveal, she was also passionately in love with her God.

Loving God

O Lord God, will to give me
All that leads me to you.
O Lord God, take away from me
All that diverts me from you.
O Lord God, take me, also, from myself
And give me completely to yourself.

Mystical Song of Love

Are you the sweet song of love and of holy awe resounding ever round God's throne triune, which unifies the pure tone of all beings within itself?

[Are you] the harmony which fits the limbs to the head, so that each blissfully finds the secret meaning of his being, and exudes it with gladness freely dissolved in your streams?

O Holy Spirit.

O Jubilation.

God's Plan

> Whatever did not fit in with my plan
> did lie within the plan of God.
> I have an ever deeper and firmer belief
> that nothing is merely an accident
> when seen in the light of God,
> that my whole life
> down to the smallest details
> has been marked out for me
> in the plan of Divine Providence
> and has a completely coherent meaning
> in God's all-seeing eyes.
> And so I am beginning to rejoice
> in the light of glory
> wherein this meaning
> will be unveiled to me.

St. Edmund

1170–1240

St. Edmund of Abingdon, archbishop of Canterbury, was a scholar, preacher, and teacher at both Oxford and Paris. Known for his holiness and his austerity, he spent much of his life in disagreement with King Henry III over foreign affairs.

But that wasn't his only problem. He also had to deal with what amounted to a revolt against him by the monks of Canterbury. When Pope Gregory once told him he would be a good monk, he replied, "Would that I could be a good monk and free from all these troubles." Finally, at the end of his life, he was granted two months of peace in a monastery.

Given all his troubles, it's no wonder his most famous prayer offers his entire day to the Lord in a classic morning offering.

Morning Offering

Into your hands, O Lord,
and into the hands of your holy angels,
I commit and entrust this day my soul,
my relations, my benefactors, my friends and my
enemies,
and all your people.
Keep us, O Lord, through this day
by the merits and intercession of the Blessed
Virgin Mary and all the saints.

St. Elizabeth Ann Seton

1774–1821

The first native-born American saint, Elizabeth Ann Seton was both a wife and mother, and the founder of today's parochial school system. Raised an Episcopalian, she married a wealthy New York merchant and had three daughters and two sons. When her beloved husband contracted tuberculosis, they traveled to Italy in search of a cure. Unfortunately, he died there, leaving his widow in the care of a Catholic family. When she returned to America, she was determined to convert, despite opposition from friends and family.

After years of struggle, she opened a girls' school in Baltimore and was joined by several other women who helped her found the American Sisters of Charity. Even while she was a mother superior, she remained a mother. She arranged for her daughters to have debutante parties, complete with ball dresses and festivities, and she continually fretted over her sons and their adventures. A woman of deep feelings, her prayers tumble from the depths of her heart.

Deliver Me from Evil

Almighty and Giver of all mercies, Father of all, who knows my heart and pities its weaknesses: you know the desire of my soul to do your will. It struggles to wing its flight to you, its Creator, and sinks again in sorrow for that imperfection which draws it back to earth. How long will I contend with sin and morality . . . Redeemer of sinners! Who gave your life to save us, assist a miserable sinner who strives with the corruption and desires above all things to break the snares of the enemy.

Short Prayers

Eternity, eternity, when shall I come to you at last? . . . In eternity where we will love with a glance of the soul.

O my soul, be fastened link by link, strong as death, iron, and Hell, as says the sacred Word.

ST. EPHRAEM THE SYRIAN

c. 306–c. 373

St. Ephraem has a unique distinction: he is the first recorded hymn writer of Christianity. While Christians undoubtedly sang songs before Ephraem came along, his are the earliest of which we have record. It is largely due to his influence that sacred songs are now an integral part of our worship.

Called the Harp of the Holy Spirit for his silver tongue, Ephraem is the only Syrian father of the church who is also honored as a Doctor of the Western church.

While his words are indeed poetic, Ephraem himself was hardly a sight to behold. He was described as being small and bald, with shriveled skin "dried up like a potsherd." He wore dirt-colored clothes. He wept much and was never seen to laugh.

Obviously, Ephraem is a good example of why we shouldn't judge a book—or a person—by its cover.

The Sacred Pearl

On a certain day a pearl did I take up, my brethren;
I saw in it mysteries pertaining to the Kingdom;
Semblances and types of the Majesty;
It became a fountain, and I drank out of it mysteries of the Son.
I put it, my brethren, upon the palm of my hand,
That I might examine it:
I went to look at it on one side,
And it proved faces on all sides.
I found out that the Son was incomprehensible,
Since He is wholly Light.
In its brightness I beheld the Bright One Who cannot be clouded,
And in its pureness a great mystery,
Even the Body of Our Lord which is well-refined:
In its undividedness I saw the Truth
Which is undivided.
It was so that I saw there its pure conception,
The church, and the Son within her.
The cloud was the likeness of her that bore Him,
And her type the heaven,
Since there shone forth from her His gracious Shining.

I saw therein his Trophies, and His victories, and His crowns.
I saw His helpful and overflowing graces,
And His hidden things with His revealed things.

For Virtues

O Lord and Master of my life,
Grant not unto me a spirit of idleness,
of discouragement,
of lust for power,
and of vain speaking.
But bestow upon me, your servant,
the spirit of chastity,
of meekness,
of patience,
and of love.
Yea, O Lord and King,
grant that I may perceive
my own transgressions,
and judge not my brother,
for blessed art you
unto ages of ages.
Amen.

St. Faustina Kowalska

1905–1938

Faustina Kowalska might have remained a rather ordinary member of the Sisters of Our Lady of Mercy except for one extraordinary occurrence: Jesus paid her a personal visit. On February 22, 1931, he appeared before her wearing a white robe and emanating two rays of light—one red and one white—from his heart. He instructed Sister Faustina to have a painting made of his image and told her he wanted the first Sunday after Easter celebrated as the Feast of Divine Mercy.

Because the course of sainthood seldom goes smoothly, it's not surprising that Faustina faced challenges in fulfilling Jesus' request. She had difficulty getting people to participate in the Divine Mercy movement. Finding an artist to do Jesus' image justice proved to be enormously frustrating.

In the end, Faustina had to settle for the best she could get. To the end of her life, she said that the picture she had painted barely represented the beauty she had experienced.

Pope John Paul II has a deep devotion to her as a fellow Pole. He made several pilgrimages to her shrine and greatly helped promulgate her Chaplet of Divine Mercy.

THE CHAPLET OF DIVINE MERCY

Jesus, I trust in you.

Recite one Our Father, one Hail Mary, and the Apostles' Creed; on the Our Father beads of the rosary, say the following:

Eternal Father, I offer you the Body and Blood, Soul and Divinity of your dearly beloved Son, Our Lord Jesus Christ, in atonement for our sins and those of the entire world.

On the Hail Mary beads say the following:

For the sake of his sorrowful passion, have mercy on us and the whole world.

At the conclusion of each decade, recite three times:

Holy God, Holy Mighty One, Holy Immortal One, have mercy on us and the whole world.

St. Frances Xavier Cabrini

1850–1917

The first American citizen to be canonized, St. Frances Cabrini arrived in New York from Italy in 1889. While thousands were pouring into the "land of promise" buoyed by optimism for a better life, Frances had reason to be disappointed—and not just because of the poverty and prejudice she encountered. Frances had longed to be a missionary to China. She had even added "Xavier" to her name after Francis Xavier, the great missionary to Asia. The United States, while certainly mission territory, wasn't quite the same as the exotic East. Never a woman to be discouraged, however, she and her companions immediately devoted themselves to serving the influx of Italian immigrants, most of whom were poor, uneducated, and often without faith.

Frances Cabrini might have thought her life was to be spent in the wilds of Wall Street, but God had other plans. From her new base in the United States, she founded communities in New Orleans, Chicago, Denver, Managua, Nicaragua, Buenos Aires, and several other locations.

One of the great ironies of her life was that she was often required to sail across the oceans as she founded her communities around the world. Because of a near-drowning experience as a child, she was terrified of water.

Bread

Bread of Heaven,
Bread of Love,
Bread of Life
shall never be lacking from God's little orphaned children.

(Said when she found a loaf of fresh-baked bread at the foot of a statue of Jesus at the opening of her first orphanage)

For Conversion

Convert me, Jesus, convert me completely to yourself, for if you do not make me a saint, I will not know how to work in your vineyard and will end by betraying your interests instead of rendering them successful.

Instrument in God's Hands

Lord, you are the one who acts. I am not even an instrument in your hands, as others say. You alone are the one who does all, and I am nothing more than a spectator of the great and wonderful works that you know how to accomplish.

Short Prayers

I thank you, dear Jesus, that your will and not mine has been done.

O Jesus, Jesus. I grieve with love for you. I am languishing and dying. Why don't I die for love of you?

St. Francis de Sales

1567–1622

The bishop of Geneva and a Doctor of the church, St. Francis de Sales was the author of numerous popular books and devotional manuals, the most famous of which is the *Introduction to the Devout Life.*

Dedicating his life to teaching the way of sanctity to ordinary men and women, St. Francis de Sales once said, "It is a mistake, a heresy, to want to exclude devoutness of life from among soldiers, from shops and offices, from royal courts, from the homes of the married."

Francis had many friends and maintained a voluminous correspondence with them. *Introduction to the Devout Life* is the result of the notes of advice he jotted to Mme. de Chamoisy, a cousin by marriage. One of his dearest spiritual companions was

St. Jane de Chantal, with whom he helped found the Order of the Visitation. When Jane, a young widow, was first contemplating a religious vocation, she appeared at a party bedecked in her family's finest jewels. St. Francis looked her up and down and then asked if she was seeking a husband or still considering religious life. When Jane assured him her heart was set on the convent, Francis wryly observed, "Then, Madame, I suggest you lower the sails."

Despite his extensive suggestions on prayer, he recorded relatively few of his own prayers, preferring to rely on the established prayers of the church, as he indicates in the following passage.

Advice on Prayer

Begin all prayer, whether mental or vocal, by an act of the Presence of God. If you observe this rule strictly, you will soon see how useful it is.

It may help you to say the Creed, Lord's Prayer, etc., in Latin, but you should also study them diligently in your own language, so as thoroughly to gather up the meaning of these holy words, which must be used fixing your thoughts steadily on their purport, not striving to say many words so much as seeking to say a few with your whole heart. One Our Father said devoutly is worth more than many prayers hurried over.

The rosary is a useful devotion when rightly used, and there are various little books to teach this. It is well, too, to say pious Litanies, and the other vocal prayers appointed for the Hours and found in manuals of devotion—but if you have a gift for mental prayer, let that always take the chief place, so that if, having made that, you are hindered by business or any other cause from saying your wonted vocal prayers, do not be disturbed, but rest satisfied with saying the Lord's Prayer, the Angelic Salutation, and the Creed after your meditation.

Morning Prayer

Lord, I lay before you my weak heart, which you fill with good desires. You know that I am unable to bring the same to good effect, unless you bless and prosper them, and therefore, O Loving Father, I entreat of you to help me by the Merits and Passion of your dear Son, to whose honor I would devote this day and my whole life.

Acceptance of All Things

O God, may your will be done, not only in the execution of your commandments, counsels, and inspirations, which we ought to obey, but also in suffering the afflictions which befall us. May your will be done in us and by us in everything that pleases you!

Short Prayers

Cast me not away from your Presence, and take not your Holy Spirit from me.

Show me your ways, O Lord, and teach me your paths.

Give me understanding, and I shall keep your Law:
I shall keep it with my whole heart.

I am your servant, O grant me understanding.

St. Francis of Assisi

c. 1181–1226

Perhaps the most famous of all saints, St. Francis of Assisi is sometimes viewed as a harmless eccentric who wandered around barefoot and dirty, talking with animals and generally being a holy hippie. Conversely, he is also seen as a paragon of piety, a man so removed from the ordinary that he never experienced normal life.

Neither view is accurate. Before his conversion, Francis was a well-to-do playboy soldier. When he embraced "Lady Poverty," it was because he had experienced the trappings of wealth and had found them wanting. When he became an ascetic, it was because he had experienced the pleasures of the flesh. When he became drunk on God, it was because he had already drained the cup of worldly pleasure and accomplishment.

While his followers were sometimes inclined to see him as incapable of sin, he himself remained keenly (and humorously) aware of his own temptations. He once told a group of people who were proclaiming him a saint, "Do not make me a saint yet, for I am still perfectly capable of fathering children."

One of Francis's most attractive attributes was his ability to recognize God in all creation. His famous "Canticle of Brother Sun and Sister Moon," written while he was suffering great agony prior to his death, gives thanks for the universe, especially for Sister Death, whose arrival Francis was anxiously awaiting.

Incidentally, the famous prayer attributed to Francis that begins "Lord, make me an instrument of your peace" was written by an Anglican cleric, not by St. Francis of Assisi. The prayer, however, eloquently reflects the essence of Francis, who practiced the spirit of the prayer even though he didn't write the words. "St. Francis's Prayer," as it is also known, actually first appeared in a religious magazine published in 1913 in Normandy, France, and was introduced to Japan after World War II.

The Canticle of Brother Sun and Sister Moon

Most High, all-powerful, all-good Lord,
All praise is yours, all glory, all honor, and all blessings.
To you alone, Most High, do they belong,
and no mortal lips are worthy to pronounce your Name.
Praised be you my Lord with all your creatures,
especially Sir Brother Sun,
Who is the day through whom you give us light.
And he is beautiful and radiant with great splendor,
Of you Most High, he bears the likeness.
Praised be you, my Lord, through Sister Moon and the stars,
In the heavens you have made them bright, precious, and fair.
Praised be you, my Lord, through Brothers Wind and Air,
And fair and stormy, all weather's moods,
by which you cherish all that you have made.
Praised be you my Lord through Sister Water,
So useful, humble, precious, and pure.
Praised be you my Lord through Brother Fire,
through whom you light the night
and he is beautiful and playful and robust and strong.

Praised be you my Lord through our Sister,
Mother Earth,
who sustains and governs us,
producing varied fruits with colored flowers and herbs.
Praise be you my Lord through those who grant pardon
for love of you and bear sickness and trial.
Blessed are those who endure in peace,
By you Most High, they will be crowned.
Praised be you, my Lord through Sister Death,
from whom no-one living can escape.
Woe to those who die in mortal sin!
Blessed are they She finds doing your Will.
No second death can do them harm.
Praise and bless my Lord and give Him thanks,
And serve Him with great humility.

Your Holy Cross

We adore you and we bless you, Lord Jesus Christ, here and in all churches which are in the whole world, because by your holy cross you have redeemed the world.

For Guidance

God Almighty, Eternal, Righteous, and Merciful, give to us poor sinners to do for your sake all that we know of your will, and to do always what pleases you, so that inwardly purified, enlightened, and kindled by the fire of the Holy Spirit, we may follow in the footprints of your well beloved Son, Our Lord Jesus Christ.

God's Greatness

You are holy, Lord, the only God and your deeds are wonderful.
You are strong.
You are great.
You are the Most High,
You are almighty.
You, holy Father, are King of heaven and earth.
You are Three and One, Lord God all Good.
You are Good, all Good, supreme Good, Lord God living and true.
You are love,
You are wisdom,
You are humility,
You are endurance,
You are rest,
You are peace.
You are joy and gladness.
You are justice and moderation,
You are all our riches, and you suffice for us.
You are beauty.
You are gentleness.
You are our protector,

You are our guardian and defender.
You are courage,
You are our haven and our hope,
You are our faith, our great consolation.
You are our eternal life, great and wonderful Lord,
God almighty, merciful Savior.

St. Gabriel Possenti

1838–1862

Gabriel Possenti should be the patron saint of procrastinators. He managed to put off entering the priesthood not once, but twice.

After a blessedly normal childhood and adolescence (something rare in saints who die young), Gabriel contracted a serious illness and promised God he would join the religious life if he recovered. He did recover and promptly put off fulfilling his promise. He got sick again, again prayed for recovery, and again promised to become a priest. Again he recovered and again he procrastinated. It wasn't until one of his sisters died that he finally got his act together and joined the Passionist novitiate under the name Gabriel-of-Our-Lady-of-Sorrows. (Maybe he took her as his patron in the hope that Mary would be more sympathetic than Jesus to his procrastination.)

By all accounts, he was a cheerful, patient, and kind novice. Like Thérèse of Lisieux, he contracted tuberculosis when he was only twenty-four, and he died before being ordained.

A Prayer for Assertion

Help me, O my God. Do help me to correct myself. This grace I ask through your own goodness, through your infinite mercy. To obtain it, I offer you the merits of Jesus Christ, our Savior and Lord. I have no merits of my own, I am destitute; but his wounds will be my plea. (Your wounds, O Lord, are my merits!) Had I shed my blood for love of you, like your son, would you not grant me this favor? How much more ought you to hear me now, since he shed his for me?

Are you not he who has promised in his Gospel whatsoever I ask for the good of my soul, you will grant: (Ask and you shall receive)? Now, as you cannot withdraw your word, I beseech you to hear me. I beseech you through your infinite goodness; through the heart of your son wounded with love for me; through the infinite charity of your eternal Spirit; through the love you bear your most holy daughter Mary; and for the honor of the whole heavenly court, into which I ask you one day to admit me. Amen.

My Jesus, I paid you ever so many little visits; do not abandon me now. O Jesus, my love!

St. Gemma Galgani

1878–1903

A woman of enormous physical and spiritual beauty, St. Gemma Galgani lived a life of piety, charity, and suffering. Although she desired to become a Passionist nun, her frail health prevented her from joining the convent. Instead she lived a frugal life in her own home. There she experienced numerous miraculous occurrences, including receiving the stigmata and the gift of prophecy.

One of her favorite saints was Gabriel Possenti. Through his intercession she was cured of complications from meningitis. She was also able to communicate directly with her guardian angel, usually in order to deliver a letter or message to her spiritual director. Often (and to the priest's amazement) the reply came via the priest's guardian angel.

Like so many other young saints, she died of tuberculosis. Her passion for Christ as well as her pain are reflected in her prayers.

To the Redeemer

My Jesus, I struggle . . . I die . . . I die because of you. Jesus, Lord of strong souls, strengthen me, purify me, make me divine. Great God, God of every sacrifice, Jesus, help me; my Redemption, God from God, come to my aid. Continually you watch over me. I thirst for you, Jesus. Do you not see how I suffer in the morning before you come to me? . . . You, Jesus, are the flame of my heart. My Jesus, I would love you with my whole being. All you saints in heaven, lend me your hearts.

Loving Jesus

O Jesus, if I but consider attentively your immense solicitude for me, how greatly should I not excel in every virtue? Pardon me, O Jesus, so much carelessness, pardon such great ignorance. My God, Jesus, my love, increated goodness, what would have become of me if you had not drawn me to yourself? Open your heart to me, open to me your sacramental breast; I open mine to you.

Short Prayers

Jesus, destroy this chain of a body, for I shall never be content until my soul can fly to you. When shall I be completely blessed in you?

If I saw the gates of Hell open and I stood on the brink of the abyss, I should not despair, I should not lose hope of mercy, because I should trust in you, my God.

St. Gertrude the Great

1256–1302

St. Gertrude was left by her parents at the famous convent at Helfta when she was about five years old. Growing up under the charge of St. Mechtilde, she probably never left the cloister. Despite her limited life experiences, her mystical travels took her to heights few of us will ever experience. Her fame has increased in recent years because of renewed interest in her *Revelations,* which recounts a series of visions and mystical experiences.

Apparently she led the life of a fairly ordinary nun until she was twenty-six. At that time she experienced a vision of Christ, who removed her fears by assuring her that salvation was near at hand by saying, "I will save you. I will deliver you. Do not be afraid." From that point on, her life was centered on the study of theology and prayer.

A woman of great intelligence, Gertrude is the patron of Latin scholars. Because few people study Latin today, it's likely Gertrude would be more than willing to intercede on the behalf of people involved in other areas of study—especially if those areas concern issues of salvation.

Gertrude's prayers reflect a woman as well grounded in the practical as in the mystical.

Union with God

How I wish, O Lord, that my soul might burn with such a fire that it might melt and be like some liquid substance, so that it could be entirely poured out into you!

I vow obedience to you because your fatherly charity allures me, your loving-kindness and gentleness attract me. In observing your will, I tie myself to you because clinging to you is lovable above everything.

Guardian Angel Prayer

O most holy angel of God, appointed by God to be my guardian, I give you thanks for all the benefits which you have ever bestowed on me in body and in soul. I praise and glorify you that you condescended to assist me with such patient fidelity, and to defend me against all the assaults of my enemies. Blessed be the hour in which you were assigned me for my guardian, my defender, and my patron. In acknowledgment and return for all your loving ministries to me, I offer you the infinitely precious and noble heart of Jesus, and firmly purpose to obey you henceforward, and most faithfully to serve my God. Amen.

St. Gregory of Nazianzus

c. 330–390

Although shy by nature, St. Gregory of Nazianzus was an eloquent speaker and preacher. Of course, he might not have had a choice. St. Basil was his best friend, and Basil was as extroverted as Gregory was introverted. As is often the case, the extrovert forced the introvert to remain in the public eye, and Basil brought Gregory with him as he used his considerable talents to combat the heresy of Arianism, which denied the divinity of Christ.

Gregory kept unsuccessfully trying to retreat to solitude through most of his life. He was close to entering a monastery at Pontus, but no! Against his wishes he was appointed bishop of Sasima. He soon left his post and returned home, where he served as coadjutor to his father, the bishop of Nazianzus. (Priestly celibacy wasn't the order of the fourth century.) From then on, solitude was a lost cause. His house became a church, and he presided over the Council of Constantinople and continued to serve as bishop. Finally, a few short years before his death, he was allowed to retire to the contemplative life he had always sought.

The Dragon Is Here Again

Alas, dear Christ, the Dragon is here again.
Alas, he is here: terror has seized me, and fear.
Alas that I ate of the fruit of the tree of knowledge.
Alas that his envy led me to envy too.
I did not become like God; I was cast out of
  Paradise.
Temper, sword, awhile, the heat of your flames
and let me go again about the garden,
entering with Christ, a thief from another tree.

Light

Be purified that you may be like lights in the world, a quickening force to all others. May you stand as perfect lights beside the great Light. And may you learn the mystery of the illumination of heaven, enlightened by the Trinity more purely and clearly.

Blessed Henry Suso

1298–1366

You may think that mystics live free of ordinary strife, but that's an illusion. Most mystics suffer terribly. Dominican Henry Suso was no exception. His many trials included severe depression and accusations of misdeeds, ranging from sacrilege and heresy to fathering a child and poisoning.

Perhaps his single greatest suffering came from the long periods of aridity in prayer, in which God seemed to have withdrawn from him completely. A close friend of Meister Eckhart, Suso is the author of the *Little Book of Eternal Wisdom,* a devotional book that has retained its popularity for more than a thousand years.

Only Jesus

I am naught, I have naught, I desire only one thing and that is our Lord Jesus, and to be with Him at peace in Jerusalem. I have nothing . . . I desire nothing but Jesus.

When Words Fail

What, my beloved, you realization of all desire, what, my beloved Lord, should I say to you while I am struck dumb with love? My heart is full of loving thoughts, if only my tongue could express them! What I experience is bottomless. What I love is endless; and therefore, what I want to say is wordless. You are my King, you are my Lord, you are my Love, you are my Joy, you are my Hour of Gladness.

Night Prayer

My soul longs for you all night, O Eternal Wisdom! And in the early morning I turn to you from the depths of my heart. May your holy presence remove all dangers from my soul and body. May your many graces fill the inmost recesses of my heart, and inflame it with your divine love.

St. Hilary of Poitiers

315–367

It's hard for moderns to get excited about the finer points of heresy. Somehow we're not easily drawn into passionate arguments over whether the Son and the Father are consubstantial. However, St. Hilary dedicated much of his life to combating this heresy, called Arianism.

St. Jerome called St. Hilary a "most eloquent man" and complained of the long, involved sentences in Hilary's dissertations. Although St. Jerome was, by all accounts, a most crabby man, his words of complaint are accurate: St. Hilary's writings are quite complex. Ironically, his prayer asks that we be kept from "vain strife of words."

Steady Faith

O Lord, keep us from vain strife of words:
Grant to us a constant
Profession of the Truth.
Preserve us in the Faith,
True Faith and undefiled,
That ever we may hold fast
That which we professed when we were Baptized
Unto, and in the Name of, the
Father, Son and the Holy Ghost.

St. Hildegard of Bingen

1098–1179

St. Hildegard, German mystic and abbess, has had a recent resurgence in popularity. Her writings, songs, medical and scientific encyclopedias, plays, poetry, and historical accounts have become best-sellers at Borders and Barnes & Noble. In fact, Hildegard has inspired many over the centuries, including such famous saints as Bernard of Clairvaux, Thomas Becket, and numerous popes.

Her collection of mystical visions, called the *Scivias,* focuses on the relationship between God and humanity. Highly critical of her times, which she called the effeminate age, she believed that God was forced to call women to do men's work, and she was determined to hold up her part of the bargain.

While she experienced the full measure of mysticism, including visions, prophecies, premonitions, and ecstasies, she was also a woman of great practicality. For instance, she made sure her convent at Bingen had running water throughout—truly a miracle in the Middle Ages!

The Branch

O budded, greening branch!
You stand as firmly rooted in your nobility
As the dawn advances.
Now rejoice and be glad;
Consider us frail ones worthy
To free us from our destructive ways:
Put forth your hand and
Raise us up.

Strength of Everlasting

Strength of Everlasting!
In your heart, you invented order. Then you spoke the word and all that you ordered was, just as you wished. And your word put on vestments woven of flesh, cut from a woman born of Adam to bleach the agony out of his clothes.
The Savior is grand and kind!
From the breath of God he took flesh!

Unfettered (for sin was not in it) to set everything
free
And bleach the agony out of his clothes.
Glorify the Father, the Spirit, and the Son.
He bleached the agony out of his clothes.

To the Handiwork of God

O handiwork of God, O human form divine!
In great holiness you were fashioned,
For the holy one pierced the heavens in great
humility.
And the splendors of God shown forth
In the slime of the earth:
The angels that minister on high see heaven
clothed in humanity.

St. Ignatius of Antioch

c. 37–107

After he was condemned by Emperor Trajan to die in the public games, St. Ignatius, the elderly bishop of Antioch, was hauled to Rome in the back of a cart. He was not idle during his trip—he preached, visited several churches on the way, met and befriended St. Polycarp, and found time to write seven letters on the faith. Not bad for a man in his seventies!

Along the way, he prayed he would not inconvenience anyone who might want to rescue his body. Apparently his prayer was answered, for tradition says he was completely devoured by the lions as soon as he was thrown into the arena.

Jesus' Wheat

Let me be food for wild beasts, for they are my way to God. I am Jesus Christ's wheat. I must therefore be ground and broken by the teeth of wild beasts that I may become his pure and spotless bread. . . . I desire and pray that the animals will not leave anything of me on the earth and that, when my spirit has flown to eternal rest, my body may not be an inconvenience to anyone.

Prayer for the Dead

Receive in tranquility and peace, O Lord, the souls of your servants who have departed this present life to come to you. Grant them rest and place them in the habitations of light, the abodes of blessed spirits. Give them the life that will not age, good things that will not pass away, delights that have no end, through Jesus Christ our Lord.

Martyr's Prayer

Blessed be the God and Father of our Lord Jesus Christ, who of his great and abundant goodness willed that I should be a partaker of the sufferings of his Christ and a true and faithful witness of his Divinity.

St. Ignatius of Loyola

1491–1556

St. Ignatius of Loyola's illustrious army career ended when a cannonball shattered his leg. While recuperating from his wounds, he had a limited choice of reading material—a romance and a lives of the saints. He chose the lives of the saints, and thereby hangs the tale: he immediately experienced a profound and life-changing conversion.

Never one to do things by halves (he had his broken leg rebroken and reset not once, but twice—without the benefit of anesthesia), he promptly dedicated his entire life to God. Once he recovered from his wounds, he went back to school in Paris, where he studied philosophy. (Perhaps he should be the patron of those who go back to school after a first career!)

Eventually, he encouraged six friends to join him as missionaries to the Muslims in Jerusalem. That dream didn't materialize, but eventually St. Ignatius founded the Jesuits, a missionary order that continues to spread the gospel throughout the world.

Prayer of Surrender

Receive, Lord, all my liberty, my memory, my understanding, and my whole will. You have given me all that I have, all that I am, and I surrender all to your divine will, that you dispose of me. Give me only your love and your grace. With this I am rich enough, and have no more to ask.

A Servant Prayer

Fill us, we pray you, with your light and life,
that we may show forth your wondrous glory.
Grant that your love may so fill our lives
that we may count nothing too small to do for you,
nothing too much to give,
and nothing too hard to bear.
Dearest Lord,
teach me to be generous.
Teach me to serve you as you deserve;
to give, and not to count the cost;
to fight, and not to heed the wounds;

to labor, and not to seek to rest;
to give of myself, and not to ask for reward,
except the reward of knowing that I am doing
  your will.
Amen.

St. Isaac Jogues

1607–1646

It has become politically incorrect to discuss the atrocities committed by native peoples, but it's hard to relate the martyrdom of St. Isaac Jogues and his companions without mentioning the cruel treatment they suffered at the hands of the Mohawk clan of the Iroquois.

St. Isaac's hands were so mutilated—the nails ripped out and the fingers literally chewed off—that he had to get special permission to celebrate Mass when he finally escaped and returned to France.

This would have been enough to make a lesser man call it quits, but sainthood is not for the fainthearted. St. Isaac returned to the New World to continue his work with the Hurons, a group that received him with greater kindness than the Mohawks. The

Iroquois, still suspicious of what they considered his evil influence, invited him to dinner. As he entered their camp, they promptly tomahawked him, cut off his head, and stuck it on a pole.

Amazingly, his prayer focuses not on his pain, but on the suffering of Christ!

Christ's Sufferings

I thank you, O good Jesus, because I have learned with some little experience what you did condescend to suffer for me on the Cross, where your most holy body was not even sustained with cords, but hung by your hands and feet, transfixed with hardest nails.

St. Jane Frances de Chantal

1572–1641

Jane lived a comfortable life as the wife of a French baron. When he died in a hunting accident, her life turned upside down. Living with her tyrannical father-in-law, she attempted to raise her four children in peace. During this period she met the man who was to become her greatest friend and ally—St. Francis de Sales.

Certainly their friendship seems to have had a heavenly origin. She received a vision of a bishop who would advise her; when she met Francis, she instantly knew him to be the man of the prophecy. Together they founded the Order of the Visitation, a community offering a spiritual way of life to women who were unsuited to the more severe ascetic orders. St. Francis de Sales said that Jane was "one of the holiest people I have ever met on this earth."

Nevertheless, Jane had her share of struggles with her family. When she finally left the family home to permanently enter the convent, her youngest (and badly spoiled) son hung onto her leg, and she had to shake him off. Perhaps she should be considered the patron saint of people with overindulged children!

Moving

Oh my God, if our souls seek you only and claim only your love, why should we be displeased if our house is changed for us, since we carry you with us and find you in places wherever we go?

Warmth in a Cold Time

O my Lord, I am in a dry land, all dried up and cracked by the violence of the north wind and the cold; but as you see, I ask for nothing more; you will send me both dew and warmth when it pleases you.

St. John Berchmans

1599–1621

If I do not become a saint when I am young, I shall never become one," said St. John Berchmans. He got his desire, dying at age twenty-two. Like St. Thérèse of Lisieux, he practiced "the little way" of faith, preferring to let daily life be his penance.

At age seventeen, he joined the Jesuits, progressing rapidly in both his studies and his piety. A man of gentle good humor, he was stricken with a mysterious illness in the summer of 1621. When the attending physician recommended that a vintage wine be used to bathe his temples, St. John quipped that it was a good thing his illness wouldn't last long, because the treatment was so expensive.

His simple prayer reveals the essence of his heart.

Teach Me to Pray

Lord, teach me how to pray. O Lord, in my meditation let a fire flame out. Open my lips, O Lord, and my mouth will declare your praise.

St. John (Don) Bosco

1815–1888

Filled with a zest for life, St. John Bosco worked tirelessly on behalf of the poor, abandoned boys in his native Italy. As a young priest, one of his favorite sayings was "Enjoy yourself as much as you like. Just keep from sin."

He used any method he could to convince boys to follow him, including juggling and joke telling, as well as that time-honored technique—providing food. Proving that honey attracts more flies than vinegar does, many boys responded positively to his loving-kindness.

As with so many other saints, John Bosco had a particular devotion to another saint; his favorite was Francis de Sales. When John Bosco founded a religious order, he called it the Salesian Order, after his patron. At the time of John Bosco's death, the Salesians had nearly a thousand priests and nine hundred sisters. John Bosco said the following prayer as he lay in bed with a severe bout of pneumonia. (He recovered.)

Prayer in Illness

Yes, Lord, if it please you, cure me. I will not refuse any work. If I can be of service to a few souls, grant, O Lord, by the intercession of your most holy Mother, to return me to such health as will not be contrary to the welfare of my soul. Please God, let me live, if it be your will.

Christmas Hymn

Let us sing with love, O Faithful
Let us sing with jubilation
God is born to us today
Our redemption
Our Salvation!

St. John Chrysostom
c. 347–407

Many people think Chrysostom is this St. John's surname. It isn't; it's a title meaning "golden mouthed." St. John was given the name because of the brilliance of his preaching. From his youngest days, he was a gifted orator, but it wasn't until he used his formidable skills to spread the gospel that his fame grew.

Not everyone loved his sermons, however. The empress Eudoxia took umbrage at his denouncement of luxury and extravagance in her court and twice had him banished to the Taurus Mountains.

Never a robust individual, he almost died when, as a young man, he tried living the monastic life in the desert. Eventually, the empress's banishment killed him. Her officials forced him to travel in bad weather, and he died on his way to the Black Sea. His words continue to exhort, encourage, and remonstrate with us today, as they did the empress.

Intercessor's Prayer

Almighty God, who has given us grace at this time with one accord to make our common supplication to you, and has promised through your well-beloved Son that when two or three are gathered in his name you will be in the midst of them: Fulfill now, O Lord, the desires and petitions of your servants as may be best for us; granting in this world knowledge of your truth and in the world to come life everlasting.

Thanksgiving

We give thanks to God that we have not sown our seed upon rocks, nor dropped it amid thorns; and that we have neither needed much time, nor long delay, in order that we might reap the harvest.

A Twenty-Four-Hour Prayer

(One for each hour of the day and night)

1. O Lord, deprive me not of your heavenly blessings;

2. O Lord, deliver me from eternal torment;
3. O Lord, if I have sinned in my mind or thought, in word or deed, forgive me;
4. O Lord, deliver me from every ignorance and heedlessness, from pettiness of the soul and stony hardness of heart;
5. O Lord, deliver me from every temptation;
6. O Lord, enlighten my heart darkened by evil desires;
7. O Lord, I, being a human being, have sinned; do you, being God, forgive me in your loving-kindness, for you know the weakness of my soul;
8. O Lord, send down your grace to help me, that I may glorify your holy Name;
9. O Lord Jesus Christ, inscribe me, your servant, in the Book of Life, and grant me a blessed end;
10. O Lord my God, even if I have done nothing good in your sight, yet grant me, according to your grace, that I may make a start in doing good;
11. O Lord, sprinkle on my heart the dew of your grace;

12. O Lord of heaven and earth, remember me, your sinful servant, cold of heart and impure, in your Kingdom;
13. O Lord, receive me in repentance;
14. O Lord, leave me not;
15. O Lord, save me from temptation;
16. O Lord, grant me pure thoughts;
17. O Lord, grant me tears of repentance, remembrance of death, and the sense of peace;
18. O Lord, grant me mindfulness to confess my sins;
19. O Lord, grant me humility, charity, and obedience;
20. O Lord, grant me tolerance, magnanimity, and gentleness;
21. O Lord, implant in me the root of all blessings: the fear of you in my heart;
22. O Lord, vouchsafe that I may love you with all my heart and soul, and that I may obey in all things your will;
23. O Lord, shield me from evil persons and devils and passions and all other lawless matters;

24. O Lord, who knows your creation and that which you have willed for it, may your will also be fulfilled in me, a sinner, for you are blessed forevermore. Amen.

St. John Eudes

1601–1680

St. John Eudes is especially remembered for three things: first, caring for victims of the plague; second, establishing rehabilitation homes for former prostitutes; and finally, helping spread the devotion of the Sacred Heart of Jesus. One might say he was a doctor who treated physical and spiritual illness by prescribing the love of Christ.

He probably was considered a little odd by his contemporaries. For instance, he once lived in a large cask in a field in order to keep from spreading the plague (apparently it worked), and he personally housed prostitutes until they could find more suitable housing. (One wonders what his family and friends said about that!)

He may have also been a little bit hyperactive. In addition to all of his other exploits, he founded a religious order (a community of secular priests), renewed the priesthood, and preached more than a hundred missions for parish renewal. He also developed the doctrinal basis for the Sacred Heart devotion and wrote a Mass and office for the celebration of the feast. When he died at age seventy-nine, it probably was from exhaustion.

When One Has a Great Need

O desire of my soul, grant me the favor I implore;
Hearken to the cry of my heart.
You know, O Lord, what I ask of you;
My heart has so often told you.

In Time of Affliction

I realize and confess, O my God, before heaven and earth, that you are just, and that I observe this suffering, and a thousand times more, for the least of my sins. That is the reason I will embrace this affliction with all my heart to the glory of your divine justice, in submission to your sacred will, in honor of the terrible sufferings you endured on earth, in satisfaction for my sins, in fulfillment of your plans that you have made about me, and as something that comes from your most amiable hands and from your heart full of love for me.

St. John of Damascus

c. 675–749

Sometimes called John Damascene, St. John is one of the greatest poets of the Eastern church. The last of the Greek fathers of the church, he entered the monastery of St. Sabas with his adopted brother, Cosmas. Most of his time was spent writing theological discourses on topics ranging from the Trinity and the real presence to the assumption of Mary.

In their spare time, the two brothers composed and sang hymns. This was not popular with their fellow monks, who thought such activity frivolous and scandalous. Fortunately for us, some of St. John's greatest hymns of praise were saved to resound through the centuries.

Easter Hymn

O Day of Resurrection!
Let us beam with festive joy!
Today indeed is the Lord's own Passover,
For from death to life, from earth to heaven
Christ has led us
As we shout the victory hymn!
Christ has risen from the dead!

May the Lord Dwell with Me

Hold dominion over my heart, O Lord: keep it as your inheritance. Make your dwelling in me, along with the Father and the Holy Spirit. Widen in me the cords of your tabernacle, even the operations of your Most Holy Spirit. For you are my God, and I will praise you, together with the Eternal Father, and our quickening Spirit, now, henceforth, and forever.

St. John of the Cross

1542–1591

St. John of the Cross stands out among all the saints named John. Author of some of the greatest spiritual poetry ever written, he was a close friend of another great saint, Teresa of Ávila. He was also a theologian, mystic, and reformer of the Carmelite Order.

Being a reformer brought him much misery. He was misunderstood and misinterpreted, arrested and imprisoned, beaten and tortured. In fact, he bore until his death the marks of the beatings he received at the order of the vicar general of the Carmelites.

His great book *Dark Night of the Soul* has entered into Christian literature as one of the most outstanding descriptions of the aridity and desolation that come when prayer brings no comfort and it appears that God has abandoned the one praying.

Prayers in the Dark Night

Pull me from this death,
my God, and give me Life.
Do not hold me so tightly
in this knot.
See how I long to see you;
my affliction is so complete.
If only I could die
because then I would not die.

Where have you hidden yourself,
and abandoned me to my sorrow, O my Beloved!
You have fled like the hart,
having wounded me.
I ran after you, crying; but you were gone.
Quench my troubles,
for no one else can soothe them;
and let my eyes behold you,
for you are their light,
and I will keep them for you alone.

St. John Vianney, the Curé of Ars

1786–1859

St. John Vianney, the parish priest in the village of Ars, France, was a man of simple means and simple tastes—he often ate only one meal a day, of boiled potatoes. Humble and modest, he possessed remarkable common sense—saying such things as the way to combat bad habits is to do their exact opposite. His approach to holiness reflected his homespun attitude toward life, yet stories of his miracles, especially his ability to recognize secret sin, continue to be told.

It is also said he was of limited intelligence because he barely passed his Latin and seminary exams. Given his amazing insight into human nature, perhaps if he had lived today he would have been diagnosed as learning disabled or dyslexic rather than dumb.

For more than thirty years he was frequently tormented by the devil. He became rather inured to the poltergeist, his noises, and his attempted violence, once saying, "The *grappin* and I are almost mates."

He died at age seventy-three, literally worn out by his personal disciplines and the constant demands of those who came to him seeking spiritual guidance.

Prayer of Love

I love you, O my God. My only desire is to love you, until the last breath of my life. I love you, O infinitely lovable God, and I prefer to die loving you rather than to live for an instant without you. I love you, O my God, and I desire only to go to heaven to have the happiness of loving you perfectly. I love you, O my God, and my only fear is to go to hell because one will not have the sweet solace of loving you there. O my God, if my tongue cannot say at all times that I love you, at least I want my heart to repeat it to you as I breathe. Ah! Do me the grace: to suffer while loving you, to love you while suffering. And, that when I die: I not only will love you, but experience it in my heart. I beg you that the closer I come to my final end, you will increase and perfect my love for you. Amen.

Prayer of the Heart

O my God, come to me, so that you may dwell in me and I may dwell in you.

Blessed Jordan of Saxony

d. 1237

All saints pray to God, but many saints also request the intercession of their fellow men and women who are on the journey to heaven. Blessed Jordan of Saxony, the second master general of the Dominican Order, prayed this prayer to his mentor, St. Dominic.

Prayer to St. Dominic

O most holy priest of God, faithful confessor, and noble preacher, St. Dominic, man chosen by the Lord, beloved and in your life pleasing to God above all others; glorious for your life, teaching, and miracles, we rejoice to have you as our gracious advocate before God. I cry out to you, whom I honor with special devotion among the saints and elect of God, in this valley of sorrow. Be compassionately present, I ask, to my sin-sick soul bereft of every virtue and grace, bound as it is by so many vices and the stain of so many sins. Be present to my wretched and unhappy soul, O blessed and happy soul of the man of God, whom Divine Grace endowed with such blessings that you not only achieved a place of happy rest, blessed refreshment, and heavenly glory for yourself, but also drew numberless others to the same beatitude through your sweet admonition, fervent preaching, and praiseworthy life. Attend then, O Blessed Dominic, and lend a compassionate ear to my voice in supplication.

Blessed Julian of Norwich

c. 1343–1423

In the land of Shakespeare and Keats, Blessed Julian of Norwich is considered the first woman of English letters. What's ironic is that we don't even know her real name. We know her only by the name of the church with which she was associated—the Church of St. Edmund and St. Julian in Norwich.

The little we know about this extraordinary mystic comes from her *Revelations of Divine Love,* reflections on her sixteen visions, which she referred to as "showings." Among her most revolutionary statements are her many references to Christ in maternal terms, including calling him "our mother entirely in everything."

Although her writings effuse joy and an unshakable peace, Julian was not a natural optimist. Early in her life she was so unhappy and despairing that she prayed for an early death. She also prayed for a profound understanding of Christ's passion, a severe illness, and the desire to forgo all sin, to love all people, and to long always for God. Although she wasn't granted a premature death, she was given her other requests.

Julian's Prayer of Confidence

All shall be well
and all shall be well
and all manner of thing shall be well.

God Alone

God, of your goodness, give me yourself, for you are enough for me.
I cannot properly ask anything less, to be worthy of you.
If I were to ask less, I should always be in want.
In you alone do I have all.

St. Julie Billiart

1751–1816

At age twenty-three, Julie Billiart's life was forever changed when someone fired a shot at her father. Although the bullet missed, the trauma of the incident caused what may have been psychosomatic paralysis in Julie. She spent the next thirty years as an invalid, twenty-two of them confined to her bed. On the fifth day of a novena to the Sacred Heart, a visiting priest told Julie, "If you have any faith, take one step in honor of the Sacred Heart." From then on, she was able to walk normally. Making up for lost time, she and her friend Frances Blin founded the Institute of Notre Dame of Namur and established fifteen convents before Julie's death. When she was admonished to take it easy, she said that if God had given her back her legs, surely he intended for her to use them.

While St. Julie undoubtedly created her own prayers, she is known to have used traditional words of the church. For instance, she prayed the Magnificat as she lay dying and used the words of the Act of Contrition to bring a dying woman peace.

She ended her life by using what strength she had left to tend to the wounded of the battle of Waterloo.

The Magnificat

(Prayed as she was dying)

My soul proclaims the greatness of the Lord; my spirit rejoices in God my Savior, for he has looked with favor on his lowly servant. From this day all generations will call me blessed: the almighty has done great things for me and holy is his name. He has mercy on those who fear him in every generation. He has shown the strength of his arm, he has scattered the proud in their conceit. He has cast down the mighty from their thrones and has lifted up the lowly. He has filled the hungry with good things, and the rich he has sent away empty. He has come to the help of his servant, Israel, for he has remembered his promise of mercy, the promise he made to our fathers, to Abraham and his children forever. Glory to the Father and to the Son, and to the Holy Spirit, as it was in the beginning, is now, and will be forever. Amen.

Act of Contrition

(Prayed at the bedside of a dying woman)

O my God, with all my heart I am sorry for having sinned against you, not because I fear the punishment my sins deserve, but because you are so good and because I owe to you everything good that I have ever had.

The Quickest Prayer of All

Le Bon Dieu!

"The Good God!"

(A typical French saying that St. Julie turned into a prayer)

St. Katharine Drexel

1858–1955

It may be easier for a camel to go through the eye of a needle than for a rich person to enter the kingdom of heaven, but as Jesus told his disciples, everything is possible with God. St. Katharine Drexel is living proof. She was a bona fide modern millionaire elevated to the ranks of sainthood.

The daughter of a nineteenth-century banker, she was raised by a devout father and a generous step-mother who taught her the importance of sacrificial giving. Their example was the first profound influence on her later life.

The second was the pope himself. At a papal audience, she asked him why he didn't send more missionaries to the African Americans and Native

Americans. He told her that if she thought that was what God wanted, perhaps she should do it herself.

After adjusting to the shock of such a suggestion, Katharine did just that. She founded the Sisters of the Blessed Sacrament for Indians and Colored People, as well as 145 missions, 12 schools for Native Americans, and 50 schools for African Americans, including Xavier University in New Orleans. During her lifetime, she distributed upwards of twenty million dollars from her fortune to fund her endeavors.

At age seventy-seven, she suffered a severe heart attack and on the advice of her doctor retired to an infirmary, where she spent the last twenty years of her life in quiet prayer and contemplation.

God's Will

Oh my God, I cannot! It is not that I want anything different from what God wants . . . I cannot believe it.

Surrender and Repentance

Lord, into your hands I commend my spirit. Oh God, relying on your infinite goodness I hope to obtain the pardon of all my sins and life everlasting through the merits of our Lord and Savior Jesus Christ. Amen.

Blessed Kateri Tekakwitha

1656–1680

Kateri Tekakwitha, the "Lily of the Mohawks," was the daughter of an Algonquin mother and a Mohawk chieftain. A Jesuit missionary baptized her when she was twenty, an event that so scandalized her family that she was forced to live in exile in a Christian village.

Like the other saintly American "flower"—Rose of Lima—Kateri subjected herself to horrendous penances, including self-flagellation, fasting, overwork, lack of sleep, and more. When she died after a lifetime of illness and self-induced suffering, her dreadfully smallpox-scarred face was said to have taken on an almost angelic appearance.

She is the first Native American to be named Blessed. While few of her words were recorded, this prayer demonstrates her overriding desire for self-sacrifice in the name of Christ.

Suffering

My Jesus, I must suffer for you; I love you, but I have offended you. It is to satisfy your justice that I am here. Vent on me, O God, your anger.

St. Leo the Great

c. 400–461

Talk about bad timing: St. Leo the Great was pope when the barbarians were literally at the gates of Rome. In 452, when Attila and the Huns were ready to swarm over Italy, Pope Leo persuaded him to back off. Three years later, when the Vandals arrived, he was not so persuasive, but he did get them to agree not to burn Rome or slay its inhabitants, even though they completely sacked the city.

He is called "the Great" because he was the first to clearly define the role of the papacy. He also formulated once and for all the doctrine of the Incarnation, which declares that Jesus was both true God and true man. "Peter has spoken through Leo" was the way the Council of Chalcedon affirmed the teaching.

Eternal Things

Grant to us, O Lord, not to mind earthly things, but rather to love heavenly things, that while all things around us pass away, we even now may hold fast those things which last forever.

St. Lutgard of Aywières

1182–1246

St. Lutgard of Aywières was a twelfth-century Cistercian sister who had the gifts of prophecy and healing. A contemporary of St. Francis and perhaps the first woman to receive the stigmata, she was also a pioneer in the devotion to the Sacred Heart of Jesus.

Her journey to the divine took some interesting twists. She entered a convent at age twelve, but this particular establishment allowed her to be courted by young swains. While one was wooing her, she had a sudden vision of Christ, who offered her his love. It was an offer she couldn't refuse; from that point on she devoted herself to almost constant prayer. She also promptly kicked her shocked suitor out of her life, calling him "fodder of death."

In addition to prayer, Lutgard also spent years fasting—seven years each for the conversion of heretics, the salvation of sinners, and the salvation of Emperor Frederick II. Her greatest and most abiding desire was to have her heart united with Christ's, as she so clearly expresses in her prayer.

Union with God

Take my heart, dear Lord. May your heart's love be so mingled and united with my heart that I may possess my heart in you. May it ever remain there safe in your protection.

St. Madeleine Sophie Barat

1779–1865

If St. Madeleine Sophie Barat had lived in the twentieth century, she might have been one of the leaders of the modern feminist movement. As it was, she was definitely radical for her time—and not just because she championed the cause of education for girls in an era when embroidery and the ability to make small talk were considered vital skills for women to have.

Her very ideas about the role of women in the world have a distinctly modern ring. She once wrote, "In this century we must no longer count on men to preserve the faith. The grain of faith that will be saved will hide itself among women. A woman cannot remain neutral in the world. She too is set for the fall and resurrection of many. How different are God's thoughts from ours!"

During her lifetime she founded boarding schools for wealthy girls, but also day schools for poorer ones. At her death, she and the members of her order, the Society of the Sacred Heart, had built more than a hundred schools throughout Europe.

When God Doesn't Seem to Answer

Dear Lord, I have been asking this of you so long.

(Prayer said as she knocked on the tabernacle door)

When a Loved One Is Dying

O my God, give her back to me! Let her stay with us. We need her. We need her!

(Prayed as her dear friend Mother Desmarquest was thought to be dying; she recovered)

Prayer for Mercy

The Cross! Souls! O Jesus, give us souls. O my God, I love you. Have mercy on me!

St. Margaret Mary Alacoque

1647–1690

Most Catholics, and many non-Catholics, are familiar with the picture of Jesus with his heart visible and surrounded by thorns and flames—the Sacred Heart. Many Catholics, especially those of a "certain age," are well acquainted with the accompanying devotional practice of receiving communion on the first Friday of each month. Far fewer realize that the devotion to the Sacred Heart began in an obscure convent at Paray-le-Monial, France.

A young nun, St. Margaret Mary Alacoque received numerous visions of Christ over an eighteen-month period. During the course of Jesus' apparitions to her, he told her not only to spread devotion to his Sacred Heart but also how and why the image of his Sacred Heart was to be displayed. The devotion spread throughout the world, and a feast for the Sacred Heart on the Friday after the octave of Corpus Christi was universally accepted. It is a remarkable achievement for a woman who was described by her contemporaries as being quiet, slow, and clumsy and who was greatly tempted to despair, vanity, and self-indulgence.

Sacred Heart

O Heart of Love,
I put all my trust in you.
For I fear all things from my own weakness,
but I hope for all things from your goodness.

Devotion to God

Had I a thousand bodies, O my God, a thousand loves and a thousand lives, I would immolate them all to your service.

St. Margaret Clitherow

c. 1556–1586

"Let them take all I have and save her, for she is the best wife in all England," begged Margaret Clitherow's husband at her trial for the crimes of harboring priests and attending Mass. His pleas were to no avail. The English courts condemned Margaret to be crushed to death by a seven-hundred-pound weight.

Margaret was a convert to the faith at a time when being a Catholic was as dangerous to your health as the plague. Persecution of Catholics was encouraged, Mass was outlawed, priests were branded traitors, and hiding a priest was a crime punishable by death.

Margaret refused to enter a plea at her trial. Had she said anything, her Protestant husband and children would have had to testify against her, a consequence she could not accept, saying, "I love my husband next to God in this world." She was martyred on Good Friday.

To the Trinity

I believe in God the Father, in God the Son, and God the Holy Ghost, in these three Persons I truly believe and that by the passion, death, and merits of Christ Jesu I must be saved.

On Her Condemnation to Death

God be thanked, all that He shall send me shall be welcome; I am not worthy of so good a death as this is: I have deserved death for my offenses to God, but not for anything that I am accused of.

Prayer at the Moment of Death

Jesu! Jesu! Have mercy on me.

St. Margaret of Cortona

1247–1297

Her early hagiographies say Margaret of Cortona led "an irregular life." She was, in fact, a wealthy man's mistress. She lived with him for nine years, bearing him a son and generally enjoying a contented if dissolute life. It all ended abruptly when he was murdered by an assassin; Margaret was led to his shallow grave by her dog.

Rejected by her family, she was finally given succor by the Franciscans at Cortona. Her change in attitude, as well as her contrition after his death, has led her to be called "the perfect penitent." Eventually she became a Franciscan tertiary and spent the rest of her life working on behalf of the poor and making reparation for her past life. Like so many other zealous women of her time, her penances were so rigorous that they endangered her health. As one of her disciplines, she would not allow herself to receive Holy Communion, believing her sacrifice was more pleasing to God than her reception would have been. She prayed the following after she was finally convinced to break her self-imposed restriction.

After Holy Communion

This morning my soul is greater than the world since it possesses you, you whom heaven and earth do not contain.

Offering to Jesus

O Lord, you are the life of my life! You are a treasure to me, without which all wealth seems utter poverty. With joy, dear Lord, I offer myself to suffer anything for love of you.

Infinite Sweetness

You know that I seek and want nothing but you, who are infinitely sweet and without whom I would feel as though I were in hell.

St. Maria Soledad Torres Acosta

1826–1887

In the midst of stories of saints who braved incredible difficulties with almost surreal serenity, it's comforting to hear about St. Maria Soledad Torres Acosta. Although she spent her life nursing the sick and comforting the dying, she was revolted by illness and utterly terrified of dead bodies. It was only through intense self-determination and the grace of God that she overcame her natural fears.

Unlike so many young women drawn to religious life, Vibiana Antonia Torres y Acosta did not grow up in poverty. Instead, she was an observant child who noticed the suffering of the poor around her and was determined to help make a difference when she grew up. To that end, she asked Fr. Miguel, pastor of one of the poorest suburbs of Madrid, if she could join his new order dedicated to nursing the poor. Frail and small of stature, Sister Maria Soledad, as she was called, was the only one of the original seven women who joined the congregation who remained in the order.

For Coworkers
My God, give me fervent servants and they will be apostles in their attendance upon the sick.

Night Prayer
O most loving heart of Jesus, I commend to you this night my heart and soul that they may rest peacefully in you. Since I cannot praise you while I sleep, may my guardian angel replace me that all my heart's beats may be so many acts of praise and thanksgiving offered to your loving heart and that of your eternal Father.

For Direction
My God, if you delay the opening of the doors of your home to me, it is because you are asking something else of me; show me your will.

Short Prayers

Let us praise God; let us bless him in everything.

Blessed be God in everything.

Heart of Jesus, protect me!

Blessed Marie Rose Durocher

1814–1849

As a young woman, Melanie Durocher longed to enter a convent, but ill health prevented her from doing so. Denied admittance to all of the congregations in her native Quebec, she became the housekeeper for her brother who was a parish priest. As her charitable work increased, she came to the attention of the bishop, who asked her to start an order of sisters devoted to teaching. Not long after, she founded the Sisters of the Holy Names of Jesus and Mary. Although she lived only six more years, her order grew, and her sisters are found in Canada, the United States, Brazil, Peru, Haiti, and Lesotho.

Deathbed Prayer of Blessed Marie Rose
My God, I cannot say, as Saint Teresa did: "To suffer or to die," but to suffer, O my God, and to do your

will; behold, that is my desire! . . . Jesus, Mary, Joseph! Sweet Jesus, I love you. Jesus, be to me Jesus.

Mary

first century

After being asked to become the mother of Jesus, Mary, a young peasant woman from Nazareth, uttered the words that have become known throughout Christendom as the Magnificat.

The Magnificat

My being proclaims the greatness of the Lord,
my spirit finds joy in God my savior.
For he has looked upon his servant in her lowliness;
all ages to come shall call me blessed.
God who is mighty has done great things for me,
holy is his name;
his mercy is from age to age
on those who fear him.
He has shown might with his arm;
he has confused the proud in their inmost thoughts.
He has deposed the mighty from their thrones
and raised the lowly to high places.

The hungry he has given every good thing,
while the rich he has sent empty away.
He has upheld Israel his servant,
ever mindful of his mercy
even as he promised our fathers,
promised Abraham and his descendants forever.

(Luke 1:46–55)

St. Mary Magdalen de' Pazzi

1566–1607

A wealthy highborn native of Florence, St. Mary Magdalen de' Pazzi was a pious child, dedicating herself to God at age ten. After entering a Carmelite convent, she experienced numerous episodes of both mystical experiences and intense suffering, including a period of aridity that tempted her to suicide, as well as months lost in prayer, during which she relived the events of Christ's passion.

Among her many spiritual gifts were the charisms of prophecy, healing, and the ability to know secret sins. The sisters in her convent were so moved by the pronouncements she made while in her ecstatic trances that they recorded them for posterity.

All Treasures

Spirit of truth,
you are the reward to the saints,
the comforter of souls,
light in the darkness,
riches to the poor,
treasure to lovers,
food for the hungry,
comfort to the wanderer;
to sum up,
you are the one in whom all treasures are contained.

Prayer to the Holy Spirit

Come Holy Spirit.
Let the precious pearl of the Father and the Word's delight come.
Spirit of truth.

Blessed Mary of Jesus Crucified

1846–1878

Blessed Mary of Jesus Crucified had an unusual prayer request. She wanted to be little like an ant or a potato or an onion because they "grow unnoticed and do good things."

Mariam Baouardy's early life was marred by tragedy. When she was three her parents died within a few days of each other. Adopted by an uncle, she moved from her native Palestine to Egypt. After refusing an arranged marriage, she was a servant in Egypt, Jerusalem, and Beirut. When the family she worked for moved to France, she went along, and it was there she entered religious life.

Mary was a woman of contradiction. Although she longed to be "nothing" and remain tucked away in prayer, she traveled to India and became the first woman to be professed a Carmelite in that country. Despite the fact that she belonged to a cloistered order, she built two convents in Palestine, serving as architect and overseer of the work. Although she was illiterate (her fellow nuns gave up trying to teach her how to read and write), she was masterful at giving spiritual counsel and guidance.

When she died following complications from a fall (she was supervising laborers at one of her convents at the time), her fellow sisters honored her with a lengthy gravestone tribute commemorating La Petite Arabe—"the Little Arab." At her beatification, Pope John Paul II sought her intercession for peace in the troubled Middle East.

For Ever and Always

> I invited the whole earth, to bless you, to serve you
> For ever and always and never to end!
> With your love my heart made one.
> I invited the entire sea to bless you, to serve you.
> For ever and always, never to end!
> I called them, invited them, little birds of the air,
> to bless you, to serve you.
> For ever and always, never to end!

I called, I invited the star of the morn.
For ever and always, never to end!
I called, I invited ungrateful man, to bless you, to serve, to praise you, and to love you,
For ever and always, never to end.

Take My Soul

My enraptured spirit contemplates all your works.
Who can speak of you, O God so great!
Omnipotent one, my soul is carried away!
His wonderful beauty delights his soul.
Who can tell what the almighty looks upon?
One look!
You who gaze at me, come to me, a little nothing.

I cannot remain here on earth, my soul longing.
Call me close to you, awaken me.
You alone, alone my God, my all.
The heavens, the earth, the sun rejoice at your name so great.
I see you, supreme goodness:
Your gaze is maternal.
My father, my mother, it is in you that I sleep,
It is in you that I breathe.
Awaken!

My soul is mad with yearning, it can do no more.
Take it.
When will we see him forever, world without end!

St. Maximilian Kolbe

1894–1941

No greater love has a man than to lay down his life for his friends." Franciscan priest St. Maximilian Kolbe went a step further. He was willing to lay down his life for a total stranger.

St. Maximilian founded *Knights of the Immaculata* magazine to help fight the evils of the modern age. An outspoken opponent of the Nazi regime, he came under intense scrutiny, was arrested, and was sent to the notorious death camp at Auschwitz. There he encouraged his fellow prisoners not to lose hope but rather to trust that God's justice would ultimately prevail.

When the commandant of the camp selected ten men to starve to death in reprisal for an escape attempt, St. Maximilian stepped forward to take the place of a man who had a wife and children. Remarkably, the SS officer agreed. After nearly two and a half excruciating weeks during which the men were forced to drink their own urine, the end finally came. When the guards entered the "block of death" on August 14, the eve of the Assumption, St. Maximilian was still alive. In an act of severe mercy, the guards killed him with an injection of carbolic acid, ironically fulfilling his lifelong desire to die on a feast of Mary.

God's Eternal Love

Who would dare to imagine that you, O infinite, eternal God, have loved me for centuries, or to be more precise, from before the beginning of the centuries?

If fact, you have loved me ever since you have existed as God; thus, you have always loved me and you shall always love me! . . .

Your love for me was already there, even when I had no existence, and precisely because you loved me, O good God, you called me from nothingness to existence! . . .

For me you have created the skies scattered with stars, for me the earth, the seas, the mountains, the streams, and all the beautiful things on earth. . . .

Still, this did not satisfy you; to show me close up that you loved me so tenderly, you came down from the purest delights of heaven to this tarnished and tear-ridden world, you lived amidst poverty, hard work, and suffering; and finally, despised and mocked, you let yourself be suspended in torment on a vile scaffold between two criminals. . . .

O God of love, you have redeemed me in this terrible, though generous, fashion! . . .

Who would venture to imagine it?

St. Mechtild

1210–1285

There are at least two saints named Mechtild, both of whom lived in the thirteenth century in Germany. To confuse things even more, both of them lived with St. Gertrude. St. Mechtildis (Mechtild) of Hackeborn-Wippra was responsible for Gertrude's upbringing, and Mechtild of Magdeburg lived years later under Abbess Gertrude.

Mechtild of Magdeburg, whose prayers are reproduced here, was originally a Beguine—a woman who lived in an informal community serving the poor but who never took formal vows. She later became a Dominican tertiary and near the end of her life moved to Gertrude's convent in Saxony.

Her great work, *The Flowing Life of the Godhead,* reflects both her desire to achieve complete union with

God as well as the lofty images of courtly love that dominated European society at the time.

She was an ascetic whose intense prayer life resulted in several heavenly visions. Her prayers, however, reflect a humble woman who was willing to offer up the all-too-earthly blindness that afflicted her in her later years.

Hymn of Praise

O Jesus, most glorious in your magnificence: I praise and bless your incomprehensible omnipotence, weak and helpless for us in the passion. I adore and glorify your unsearable wisdom, accounted foolishness for us.

I praise and magnify your unutterable love, which submitted to hatred of all people for the sake of your elect. I praise and extol your meek and gentle mercy, sentenced to so fearful a death for humankind. I praise and I adore your ravishing sweetness, embittered for us by your most bitter death.

Prayer for Faithfulness

Lord, since you have taken all that I had of you, yet of your grace, leave the gift that every dog has by nature: that of being true in my distress, when I am deprived of all consolation. This I desire more fervently than your heavenly kingdom!

Prayer for Ardor

Ah, dear love of God, always embrace this soul of mine, for it pains me above all things, when I am separated from you. Oh, love, do not allow me to grow cool, for all my works are dead when I can feel you no longer.

Blessed Miguel Pro

1891–1927

If ever there were an unlikely candidate for sainthood, it would be Blessed Miguel Pro. The stories of his growing-up years are filled with anecdotes of mischief. Once, he mixed up the letter he was sending to his non-Catholic girlfriend with one intended for his mother. Needless to say, the romance was promptly curtailed. Another time, he leaned out of a window to help his sister capture her escaped canary, and much to his chagrin, the cigarettes he had in his pocket fell directly on his father, who did not buy the excuse Miguel created on the spot.

Miguel joined the Jesuits at age twenty and was ordained in Belgium because all the seminaries in Mexico had been closed under orders of the vehemently anticlerical government. He had been back home only a few weeks when President Calles banned all public worship. Miguel managed to avoid detection for several months until a young boy betrayed him. Sentenced along with his brother to execution by firing squad, he asked only that he be allowed to spend a few minutes in prayer before his execution and to die with his arms outstretched in the shape of a cross. His dying words, "Long live Christ the King," resonate in all who live and die for their faith.

Prayer When God Seems Far Away

O Lord, your empty tabernacles mourn
while we alone upon our Calvary
as orphans, ask you, Jesus, to return
and dwell again within your sanctuary. . . .
O Lord, why has your presence from us fled?
Do you not remember how in days gone by
those countless hearts which in their trials bled
found comfort in the light that from you shone? . . .
By the bitter tears of those who mourn their dead,
by our martyrs' blood for you joyfully shed,
by the crimson stream with which your heart has
  bled,
return in haste to your dear sanctuary.

St. Patrick

c. 389–c. 461

St. Patrick has a secret: Although he is inexorably associated with Ireland and is the patron of all things Irish, he was actually a Roman of British origin. He was also the son of a deacon and the grandson of a priest. Fortunately, priestly celibacy wasn't a law at the time!

Patrick might have been just another obscure Romano-Briton except for a stroke of bad luck. When he was about fourteen, he was captured by raiders and shipped to Ireland as a slave. Needless to say, he wasn't thrilled with captivity, and after six years, he ran away. He reached Gaul (ancient France), but eventually returned to the place of his birth, near Hadrian's Wall.

Several years later he went back to Ireland to spread the message of Christ to the native Irish. In a time when few people could read and write, his prayer "The Breastplate of St. Patrick" reflects his desire to become a living gospel to all he encountered.

The Breastplate of St. Patrick

I arise today
Through a mighty strength, the invocation of the Trinity,
Through a belief in the Threeness,
Through a confession of the Oneness
Of the Creator of creation.

I arise today
Through the strength of Christ's birth and his baptism,
Through the strength of his crucifixion and his burial,
Through the strength of his resurrection and his ascension,
Through the strength of his descent for the judgment of doom.

I arise today
Through the strength of the love of cherubim,
In obedience of angels,

In service of archangels,
In the hope of resurrection to meet with reward,
In the prayers of patriarchs,
In preachings of the apostles,
In faiths of confessors,
In innocence of virgins,
In deeds of righteous men.

I arise today
Through the strength of heaven;
Light of the sun,
Splendor of fire,
Speed of lightning,
Swiftness of the wind,
Depth of the sea,
Stability of the earth,
Firmness of the rock.

I arise today
Through God's strength to pilot me;
God's might to uphold me,
God's wisdom to guide me,
God's eye to look before me,
God's ear to hear me,
God's word to speak for me,
God's hand to guard me,
God's way to lie before me,
God's shield to protect me,
God's hosts to save me

From snares of the devil,
From temptations of vices,
From every one who desires me ill,
Afar and anear,
Alone or in a multitude.

I summon today all these powers between me and evil,
Against every cruel, merciless power that opposes my body and soul,
Against incantations of false prophets,
Against black laws of pagandom,
Against false laws of heretics,
Against craft of idolatry,
Against spells of women and smiths and wizards,
Against every knowledge that corrupts man's body and soul.

Christ shield me today
Against poison, against burning,
Against drowning, against wounding,
So that reward may come to me in abundance.
Christ with me, Christ before me, Christ behind me,
Christ in me, Christ beneath me, Christ above me,
Christ on my right, Christ on my left,
Christ when I lie down, Christ when I sit down,
Christ in the heart of every man who thinks of me,
Christ in the mouth of every man who speaks of me,

Christ in the eye that sees me,
Christ in the ear that hears me.

I arise today
Through a mighty strength, the invocation of the
  Trinity,
Through a belief in the Threeness,
Through a confession of the Oneness
Of the Creator of creation.

St. Philip Neri

1515–1595

Bubbling over with mirth, St. Philip Neri often quipped that his favorite two books were the Bible and a joke book. He told his disciples, "If you want to be obeyed, don't make commandments."

He wasn't lighthearted about the spiritual life, however. For nearly fifty years, he tirelessly evangelized the people of Rome, bringing the gospel to everyone from beggars to cardinals. For his efforts he is sometimes called the Second Apostle of Rome.

By the way, he is one of only a few saints who are known to have kept a cat for a pet. When the archbishop would send Philip on an assignment, he would leave the cat in the care of the archbishop, who apparently was not an ailurophile.

Although his short prayers have a jocular quality, they demonstrate the heartfelt desire for holiness that shaped his life.

Witty Prayers

O Jesus, watch over me always, especially today, or I shall betray you like Judas.

Lord, the wound in your side is large, but if you do not keep your hand on me I shall make it larger.

Lord, I will no longer promise to change my life and do better, since I promise it and do not do it.

Dedication to Jesus

My Jesus, I wish to do nothing but your most holy will. My Jesus, if you would have me, clear away all the hindrances which keep me from you. I would to serve you, my Jesus, and I do not know how. I do not know you, my Jesus.

Venerable Pierre Toussaint

c. 1776–c. 1863

A slave by birth, Ven. Pierre Toussaint was brought to New York from his native Haiti just after the Revolutionary War. Having learned the trade of hairdressing, he was able to support his mistress when she fell on hard times. He even acted as a lowly servant at her parties. On her deathbed, she granted him his freedom although he could have purchased it many times over.

Pierre raised funds for building St. Patrick's Cathedral even though, as a black man, he would never be recognized by New York society. However, at his funeral, one mourner said, "I have known Christians who were not gentlemen and gentlemen who were not Christians. I known one man who is both, and that man is black." High tribute indeed in a time when skin color alone determined one's state in life.

Prayer as One Lays Dying

God is with me, I want nothing on the earth.

St. Polycarp

c. 69–c. 155

As is the case with so many of the early saints, we know little about Polycarp except for the few details of his martyrdom. We know that he had personal contact with the Twelve and was probably installed as bishop of Smyrna by St. John. We also know that he didn't mince words, once calling the heretic Marcion "the firstborn of Satan" to his face. And we know that he spent most of his adult life combating heresy and teaching truth. The rest is lost in the annals of heaven.

Shortly after returning to Smyrna from Rome, where he had been helping to set the date for Easter, eighty-six-year-old St. Polycarp was sentenced to be burned alive when he refused to recant his faith. The fire would not consume him and instead surrounded him. As the martyrology says, he was "like gold and silver being purified in a smelting furnace." Polycarp was then stabbed to death.

His prayer is one of the oldest prayers of the church. It is modeled after the prayers that would have been said each Sunday during the liturgical services.

Martyr's Prayer

O Lord God Almighty, Father of your blessed and beloved son Jesus Christ, through whom we have been given knowledge of you; you are the God of angels and powers, of the whole creation, and of all the generations of the righteous who live in your sight. I bless you for granting me this day and hour, that I may be numbered among the martyrs, to share the cup of your Anointed and to rise again to life everlasting, both in body and soul, in the immortality of the Holy Spirit. May I be received among them this day in your presence, a sacrifice rich and acceptable, even as you did appoint and foreshow, and now bring to pass, for you are the God of truth and in you there is no falsehood. For this, and for all else besides, I praise you, I bless you, I glorify you through our eternal High Priest in heaven, your beloved son Jesus Christ, by whom and with whom be glory to you and the Holy Spirit, now and for all ages to come.

St. Prisca

first century

While little is known about St. Prisca, we do know she was one of many courageous men and women who were willing to suffer death during the persecutions of ancient Rome rather than worship a false god. Her prayer, said just before her execution, is a reflection of her immortal faith and her all-too-mortal fear.

Prayer at Her Execution

O Lord God, Eternal King! You who stretched out the heavens and built the earth. You who put limits on the ocean and trampled the Serpent's head. You, O Lord, do not abandon me now. Hear my prayer.

Blessed Richard Rolle

c. 1300–1349

Although he is considered one of the shining lights of medieval mystics, Blessed Richard Rolle doesn't seem to have had "usual" mystical experiences such as levitation, visions, trances, and the like. In fact, he was eminently ordinary, taking special delight in offering spiritual counsel to women religious and writing extensively on practical Christian life.

His journey to sainthood began when he dropped out of Oxford and began to live as a hermit, using one of his sister's dresses to create a makeshift habit. (Understandably miffed, she thought he had gone crazy.) He spent the rest of his life more or less alone until he died of the plague.

Anyone who would brave his sister's wrath to dismantle one of her dresses would have to have a sense of humor, and Richard did. He viewed righteous laughter as mirth suitable to the love of God. His prayer is typical of medieval religious sentiment and piety.

Lover's Song

O honey sweet heat, than all delight sweeter, than all riches more delectable. O my God! O my Love! into me glide; with your charity thrilled; with your beauty wounded: Slide down and comfort me, heavy; give medicine to me, wretched; show yourself to your lover. Behold in you is all my desire, and all my heart seeks. After you my heart desires; after you my flesh thirsts. And you open not to me but turn your Face. You spar your door, and hide yourself; and at the pains of the innocent you laugh.

In the meantime nevertheless you ravish your lovers from all earthly things; above all desire of worldly things you take them, and make them takers of your love and full great workers in loving. Wherefore in ghostly song, of burning up bursting, to you they offer praises, and with sweetness they feel the dart of love.

Hail therefore O lovely Everlasting Love, that raises us from these low things and presents us with so frequent ravishings to the sight of God's Majesty. Come into me, my Beloved! All that I had I gave for you, and that I should have, for you I have forsaken, that you in my soul might have a mansion for to comfort it. Never forsake you him that you feel so sweetly glow with desire for you; so that with most burning desire I desire, to be ever within your hands. So grant me grace to love you, and in you to rest, that in your kingdom I may be worthy for to see you without end.

St. Richard of Chichester

1197–1253

St. Richard undoubtedly would be the first to say that getting on the wrong side of a monarch is a bad idea. Richard fell under the wrath of King Henry III when Henry wanted one of his own toadies elevated to the position of bishop of Chichester. Unfortunately for Henry, St. Richard was already the bishop of Chichester. Since a king is seldom thwarted, St. Richard was reduced to a virtual outcast in his own diocese. He could have become bitter and angry, but as his famous prayer demonstrates, he refused to focus on his misfortune, concentrating always on his gratitude. Words from this prayer made their way into the song "Day by Day" from the musical *Godspell*.

Gratitude

Thank you, Lord Jesus Christ,
For all the benefits and blessings
Which you have given me,
For all the pains and insults
Which you have borne for me.
Merciful Friend, Brother and Redeemer,
May I know you more clearly,
Love you more dearly,
And follow you more nearly,
Day by day.

Prayer for Mercy

You know, Lord, that if it be pleasing to you I am ready to bear all insults and torments and even death for you. Therefore, as you know this to be the truth, have mercy on me now, for to you I commit my soul.

St. Rita of Cascia

1381–1457

St. Rita should be named the patron saint of abused women. Her parents arranged her marriage to a man who turned out to be a classic abuser. Not only was he a brutal, unfaithful drunk, but his temper was so violent that the entire neighborhood was afraid of him. That Rita could or would put up with him might have been enough to assure her sanctity, but her faithful kindness apparently caused him to see his faults and to beg her forgiveness shortly before he was murdered.

One of St. Rita's requests is not something most of us would pray for. When she saw that her sons were following in their father's violent footsteps, she prayed that they would die before they sinned. Both sons immediately fell victim to a fatal illness!

Freed from the responsibilities of marriage and parenthood, Rita then tried to join the convent at Cascia. Three times she was rebuffed for not being a virgin, but Rita was persistent. The rules were eventually changed to accommodate her.

Prayer on Her Casket

Blessed by God, you were a light in darkness through your steadfast courage. When you had to suffer such agony upon your cross, you turned aside from the vale of tears to seek wholeness for your hidden wounds in the great passion of Christ. . . . You were not content with less than perfect healing, and so endured the thorn for fifteen years before you entered into the joy of your Lord.

Patience

O loving Jesus, increase my patience according as my sufferings increase.

Rose Hawthorne Lathrop

1851–1926

Most people are familiar with the novelist Nathaniel Hawthorne, author of *The House of the Seven Gables.* Fewer know that the Unitarian Hawthorne had a daughter who not only converted to Catholicism but was a founder of a religious order.

Born to a life of privilege—her father was the American consul to England as well as a literary light—Rose traveled extensively in her youth. Once, while visiting the Vatican gardens, she literally bumped into a praying priest who turned out to be Pope Pius IX! At age twenty she married George Lathrop, an aspiring writer. The marriage turned out to be a disaster. Their only son died of diphtheria and George became an alcoholic. His drinking became so intolerable that Rose applied for and received permission from her bishop to leave her husband, an almost unthinkable action at the time.

After George's death, Rose determined to dedicate her life to God. Thus, at age forty-four, she embarked on a new career—nursing the sick and destitute. The remaining years of her life were spent as Sister Alphonsa, foundress of the Dominican Servants of Relief for Incurable Cancer. Her prayer reflects her determined, forthright, and straightforward nature.

Asking Boldly

Lord, you must give us this new house. We need it. And I have nobody to look to but you, dear Lord!

(Said as she requested a new home for members of her religious order)

St. Rose of Lima

1586–1617

St. Rose of Lima, the first canonized saint of the Americas, was a little odd, even by saintly standards. If she were alive today, she probably would receive psychological counseling for bulimia, self-mutilation, and general mental instability. Fortunately for her sainthood, she lived in the seventeenth century, a time when excessive mortification was seen as the piety she intended it to be.

Born in Lima, Peru, she was named Isabel and took the name Rose at confirmation. When her family fell on hard times, she helped support them by growing flowers and doing embroidery work, even after she dedicated her life to God as a member of the Third Order of St. Dominic. In addition, she opened her parents' home to anyone who was sick, emulating her Peruvian compatriot St. Martin de Porres.

Eventually her family could no longer tolerate her excesses, such as scarring her face with hot pepper and regularly flogging herself until she bled, so she moved to the home of a friend, where she died after a lingering illness. Her prayer reflects the passion of her soul.

Passion for God

Oh my God! Who would not love you? O good Jesus! When will I begin to love you as I am obliged? How far am I from this perfect, intimate, and generous love? Alas! I know not even how to love you. How shameful! What advantage is it to have a heart, unless it be quite consumed with love for you!

During a Time of Aridity in Prayer

Alas, my only true love has vanished;
From his favor I am banished.
Gone that smile which flashed so bright.
Gone my heart's once radiant light.
How could he leave me?
Did his promise deceive me?
Ah no! He will return.
Soon, soon my heart will burn!

Come you, my pleasure,
And I shall love you without measure.

St. Rose Philippine Duchesne

1769–1852

Never give up! should be the motto of St. Rose Philippine Duchesne. She longed to be a missionary to Native Americans and prayed regularly to be allowed to enter the mission field, but she was seventy-two years old before her prayer was answered.

Young Rose Philippine joined religious life in 1788, but her community was dispersed by the French Revolution, and her father, who never liked the idea of her being a nun anyway, forced her to return home. After the revolution, she tried to restore the convent she had originally joined, which had been decimated by the revolution, but was unsuccessful in getting her former sisters to join her. Finally, she entered St. Madeleine Sophie Barat's Society of the Sacred Heart.

St. Madeleine helped her learn to accept the will of God for her life, and finally, when she was forty-nine, she received permission to emigrate to America with four other sisters. There she did her best to educate pioneer children, but she continued to pray to be allowed to minister to the Native Americans. Her prayer was answered when she was sent to Sugar Creek, Kansas, to establish a school for young girls. To her sorrow, she was unable to master the Potawatomi language. Although she was unable to speak with them, she was much loved by the Native Americans, who called her Woman Who Prays Always.

After a scant year in Kansas, she was recalled to the American motherhouse in Missouri, where she spent the last years of her life in prayer.

Missionary's Prayer

You will go over the Jordan this day . . . say not in your heart, "For my justice has the Lord brought you to possess this land," take heed and beware, lest at any time you forget. . . . May God bless and confirm our resolution never to forget all that He has done for us.

St. Stephen

first century

The death of St. Stephen, the first Christian martyr, is recorded in the Acts of the Apostles. According to St. Luke's account, Stephen was stoned to death by a band of zealots led by a young man named Saul, one day to be known as St. Paul. As he was dying, St. Stephen, like Jesus, asked God to forgive his attackers.

Stephen was a young Hellenistic Jew chosen by the Twelve to be a deacon in Jerusalem. When he began zealously preaching the gospel, some other Jews debated him and lost because "they could not withstand the wisdom and the spirit with which he spoke." He was accused of blasphemy, his attackers saying that he was attempting to destroy the customs that Moses had handed down. When Stephen vehemently defended his beliefs, he signed his death warrant.

The First Martyr's Prayer

Lord Jesus, receive my spirit! Lord, do not hold this against them.

St. Symeon the New Theologian

949–1022

The greatest of the Byzantine mystical writers, St. Symeon was forced into exile in Asia Minor. A mystic and a poet, he used his considerable literary talents to create prayers that are both profound in their theological insights and breathtaking in their beauty.

This prayer asks the timeless questions put forth by all who struggle to know God, echoing in some ways the prayers of his spiritual father, Job.

God's Majesty

How are you at once the source of fire,
how also the fountain of dew?
How at once burning and sweetness,
how a remedy for all corruption?
How do you make gods of us men,

how do you make darkness light?
How do you make one reascend from hell,
how do you make us mortals imperishable?
How do you draw darkness to light,
how do you triumph over night?
How do you illumine the heart?
How do you transform me entirely?
How do you become one with men,
how do you make them sons of God?
How do you burn them with your love,
how do you wound them without a sword?
How can you be patient, how can you endure?
How do you not remunerate at once?
How do you see the actions of all,
you who dwell beyond all creatures?
How do you look at the conduct of each one,
you who are so far from us?
Give patience to your servants,
so that trials may not overwhelm them!

St. Teresa of Ávila

1515–1582

Charming, witty, determined, candid, outspoken, passionate—these are but a few of the qualities of St. Teresa of Ávila. One of only two women named Doctors of the church (Catherine of Siena is the other), St. Teresa experienced mystical visions and miraculous events, but she also often talked with God in an almost conversational tone, frankly speaking her mind on a variety of topics. One time the donkey she was riding got stuck in the mud crossing a river. "If this is how you treat your friends," she told God, "it's no wonder you have so few of them."

An eminently practical woman, she warned the nuns in her convent who talked about their own mystical experiences to make sure they got adequate rest and ate enough before declaring their experiences to be from God. Her vibrant good humor emerges in many of her sayings, including "God and chocolate are better than God alone!"

Teresa was not a saint from childhood. She joined a convent, but "played" at the spiritual life until she was about forty, when she had a profound and life-changing mystical conversion. From then on she lost no time. She wrote extensively, helped found seventeen new convents, and is considered, along with St. John of the Cross, one of the reformers of the Carmelite Order. Her "Bookmark" is one of the most famous prayers ever written.

For Deliverance

From silly devotions and sullen saints, deliver me, O Lord.

Govern All by Your Wisdom

Govern all by your wisdom, O Lord, so that my soul may always be serving you as you will and not as I choose. Do not punish me, I beseech, by granting that which I wish or ask, if it offend your love which would always live in me. Let me die to myself that I may serve you. Let me live to you who in yourself are the true life.

Bookmark of St. Teresa

Let nothing disturb you,
nothing frighten you,
all things are passing;
Patient endurance
attains all things:
one who God possesses
wants nothing,
for God alone suffices.

For God's Aid

O my God, my King!—I can do nothing, unless your empty hand, unless your heavenly power, assist me. With your aid, I can do all.

God's Will Be Done

Lord, grant that I may always allow myself to be guided by you, always follow your plans, and perfectly accomplish your holy will. Grant that in all things, great and small, today and all the days of my life, I may do whatever you may require of me. Help me to respond to the slightest prompting of your grace, so that I may be your trustworthy instrument, for your honor. May your will be done in time and eternity—by me, in me, and through me.

Mother Teresa of Calcutta

1910–1997

A tiny, stooped figure in a blue-and-white sari, Mother Teresa of Calcutta may be one of the most recognizable figures of the twentieth century. Her very name has become synonymous with selfless charity and compassion for the poor.

Although she is not an official saint—yet—Mother Teresa's work among the poorest of the poor in India, as well the phenomenal spread of her order, the Sisters of Charity, has caused the press to elevate her to sainthood by acclamation.

Ironically, this great symbol of Christian compassion died the same week as another icon of the modern world—Princess Diana of Wales. Anyone watching the news reports must have been struck by the differences between these two women.

It Doesn't Matter

Man is unreasonable, illogical, egocentric.
It doesn't matter—love him.
If you do good, you'll be accused of egotistic meanings.
It doesn't matter—do good.
If you realize your dreams, you'll find false friends and real enemies.
It doesn't matter—realize them.
The good you do will be forgotten tomorrow.
It doesn't matter—do good.
Honesty and sincerity make you vulnerable.
It doesn't matter—be honest and sincere.
All that you constructed in years could be destroyed in one second.
It doesn't matter—construct.
If you help people, they will resent it.
It doesn't matter—help them.
Give the world the best of you and the world will kick you.
It doesn't matter—give the best of you.

Short Prayers

O Lord God, give me grace this very day really and truly to begin, for what I have done till now is nothing.

O God, because of my free choice and for the sake of your love alone, I want to remain here and do what your will demands of me. No, I will not turn back.

St. Teresa Margaret of the Sacred Heart

1748–1770

Saints seem to congregate in the same areas. At age seventeen, Anna Maria Redi entered the Carmelite convent in Florence, Italy, where St. Teresa of Ávila once lived. As Theresa Margaret of the Sacred Heart, she spent five short years giving herself to Christ in prayer and ministering to her fellow sisters. While such a brief life might be thought of as tragic, St. Theresa Margaret felt it to be complete, once saying, "God helps us so that at journey's end, everything is finished." Her prayer is as beautiful as it is simple.

To Persevere in Love

I want to love you, O my God, with a love that is patient, with a love that abandons itself wholly to you, with a love that acts, and most important of all, with a love that perseveres.

St. Thérèse of Lisieux

1873–1897

The Little Flower, as she is often called, is one of the most popular and most loved saints of the modern era. Ironically, she became a saint not by performing great miracles, but by doing little things with great love.

Thérèse was the last of nine children of a pious couple, Louis and Zélie Martin. Her mother died when she was four, an event that left her insecure and devoted to her father. When her eldest sister, Pauline, whom she considered a "second mother," entered the Carmelites, Thérèse desired to follow her. She was so intent that when she was fifteen, she personally begged Pope Leo XIII to bend the rule that restricted entry until age sixteen and to command the superior who had forbidden her entry until she was twenty-one to let her in.

Undoubtedly stunned, Pope Leo told her to follow the proper procedures. When she again begged him, he replied, "You will enter if God wills it" and then had the Swiss guards remove her.

Apparently God did will it; Thérèse was allowed to become a Carmelite at her sister's convent within a few months. She spent the rest of her life perfecting her "little way"—putting up with frustrating companions, obeying superiors, finishing the laundry. So ordinary did she appear that some of the sisters in her convent were unaware of her remarkable prayer life until after her death. She was only twenty-four when she died of tuberculosis.

Only to Love You

My life is an instant,
a fleeting hour.
My life is a moment,
which swiftly escapes me.
O my God, you know that
on earth I have only today
to love you.

Infinite Love

O my divine Master! I cried from the bottom of my heart, is it your justice alone that will receive victims of holocausts? Has not also your merciful love need of them? Everywhere it is misunderstood, rejected. . . . The hearts upon which you long so generously to bestow it, turn aside to creatures and, for the miserable pleasure of an instant, ask happiness from them, instead of throwing themselves into your arms and accepting the sweet torrent of your infinite love.

Only for Today

Oh! how I love you, Jesus! my soul aspires to you—
And yet for one day only my simple prayer I pray!
Come reign within my heart, smile tenderly on me,
Today, dear Lord, today.
But if I dare take thought of what the morrow
  brings—
That fills my fickle heart with dreary, dull dismay;
I crave, indeed, my God, trials, and sufferings,
But only for today!

To Mary, Our Lady of Victories

O Mother! you have granted my heart's desire
So now hear my cry
Of gratitude and love like fire;
Your child lifts you on high.

By love for God and all humanity,
By bonds of prayer and earnest will,
You deign my soul to bind now
With those who fulfill Christ's last desire.
They will go to pagan lands
To raise the cross of Christ on high;
I, within the humble cloister,
Will satisfy his slightest will.

With such desire I long for suffering and crave the cross.
If I can help to save but one soul,
I'll count a thousand deaths as gain, not as loss.
For this I've come to Carmel's hill,
To immolate myself for men.
Christ brought a fire from Heaven's highest dome;
I would light his fire in hearts.
In Africa where the sun bakes the desert,
In Asia which faces east,
My Mother, I can help to make
Your virginal name revered and blessed.

Every day my prayers will travel
As fast as a mighty river rolls.
I will help my brothers [missionaries] who are commissioned far away,
To conquer souls.
And so the pure baptismal stream

Will make many a pagan child
Into a temple, where God's grace will shine
And God be reconciled with man.

Ah! If I could but see those dear children fill
The heavenly courts where seraphs sing!
By my prayers and God's sweet will,
My brothers will bring them to Jesus.
The palm my spirit desires to gain,
Will be placed by my brother's hand in mine.
A martyr's sister! Any pain
Would seem delight to win that grace.

The fruit of our apostolate
Our longing eyes will see at last
When, as we enter heaven's gate,
Our souls will meet those who were saved
And will also meet you.
May the honor of my priestly brothers' fight
So far away, be mine also,
May mine be a reflection of their light,
At last in the eternal day of heaven.

To Joan of Arc

Joan, from heaven remember your homeland,
Remember all her flower-covered valleys,
Recall her smiling plains, her mountains so grand.
In other hours you left to dry her tears.
Remember how your arm saved France from the
enemy.

Remember, O angel sent from heaven, how you cured her woes.
Now again France calls on you in her night of pain.
Remember!

Remember those great victories you won at Rheims and Orleans,
Remember those days when you did great deeds in the name of God,
Crowning your homeland with laurels and honor.
Now, far away from you, I suffer and I sigh.
Once you died for me, now come again to save me.
Deign now to break my chains,
And destroy all my present pains.
Remember!

My arms are fettered in chains;
I cry out to you.
My eyes are veiled with tears;
Oh give me solace!
I am not one of earth's great queens
And my children break my heart.
They care no more for God,
They despise even their mother.
O Joan, be compassionate toward my many miseries.
Daughter of noble heart,
Come and be at my side.
I hope in you.

The Holy Face

Jesus, who in your bitter passion did become "the reproach of men and the Man of Sorrow," I venerate your Holy Face on which shone the beauty and gentleness of Divinity. In those disfigured features I recognize your infinite love, and I long to love you and to make you loved. May I behold your Glorious Face in heaven!

Morning Prayer

O my God! I offer you all my actions of this day for the intentions and for the glory of the Sacred Heart of Jesus. I desire to sanctify every beat of my heart, my every thought, my simplest works, by uniting them to its infinite merits; and I wish to make reparation for my sins by casting them into the furnace of its merciful love.

For Grace to Carry On

O my God! I ask of you for myself and for those whom I hold dear, the grace to fulfill perfectly your holy will, to accept for love of you the joys and sorrows of this passing life, so that we may one day be united together in heaven for all Eternity. Amen.

Thomas à Kempis

c. 1380–1471

Best known as the author of *The Imitation of Christ,* Thomas à Kempis took as his motto "Everywhere I have sought rest and found it nowhere, save in tiny nooks with tiny books." He was born in Cologne and studied at the school of the Brothers of the Common Life. Eventually he entered a monastery where his brother was prior. He remained there the rest of his life, writing, preaching, copying manuscripts, and imitating Christ.

My Hope and My Crown

O Lord God, Holy Father, be you now and forever blessed.
For as you will, so it has been done; and what you do is good.
Let your servant rejoice in you,
not in myself or any other.

You alone are my hope and my crown.
You are my goodness and my honor.
O Lord, what does your servant have but what has been received from you
without deserving it?
Yours are all things that you have been given and have made.

Jesus' Words

These are all your words, O Christ, eternal Truth, though they were not all spoken at one time nor written together in one place. And because they are yours and true, I must accept them all with faith and gratitude. They are yours and you have spoken them; they are mine also because you have spoken them for my salvation. Gladly I accept them from your lips that they may be the more deeply impressed in my heart.

The Eucharist

Oh, how sweet and kind to the ear of the sinner is the word by which you, my Lord God, invite the poor and needy to receive your most holy Body!

Who am I, Lord, that I should presume to approach you? Behold, the heaven of heavens cannot contain you, and yet you say: "Come, all of you, to Me."

What means this most gracious honor and this friendly invitation? How shall I dare to come, I who am conscious of no good on which to presume? How shall I lead you into my house, I who have so often offended in your most kindly sight?

Angels and archangels revere you, the holy and the just fear you, and you say: "Come to Me: all of you!" If you, Lord, had not said it, who would have believed it to be true? And if you had not commanded, who would dare approach?

St. Thomas Aquinas

1225–1274

One of the greatest minds the Western world has ever produced, Dominican friar St. Thomas Aquinas is a key figure in the development of Christian theology. Called "the Dumb Ox" by his classmates in Paris, St. Thomas is the author of the greatest single work on faith ever written, the *Summa theologica*.

St. Thomas had the misfortune of being born into a family of snobs. While they were happy to have him enter religious life, they wanted him to be a Benedictine so that he might rise to the position of abbot of the prestigious Monte Cassino abbey. They were so determined to have him be an "illustrious" religious instead of a Dominican that they imprisoned him for a year in the family castle, doing everything from sending in a prostitute to tempt him to depriving him of basic necessities to get him to change his mind. He eventually escaped and joined his chosen order despite the fact that his family considered them beggars.

A year before his death, he was granted a vision that convinced him to lay aside his quill forever. The only clue to the experience was his saying, "All I have written seems to me like straw compared to what I have seen and what has been revealed to me."

His prayers are among the most well-known written by the saints.

Prayer before Study or Reading

Grant to me, O merciful God, that I might ardently love, prudently ponder, rightly acknowledge, and perfectly fulfill all that is pleasing to you, for the praise and glory of your Name.

Prayer before Lecturing, Writing, or Preaching

Ineffable Creator, from the treasure house of your Wisdom you have created the three Angelic Hierarchies. In marvelous order you established them above the Empyrean Heaven, and splendidly arranged all the parts of creation.

I ask you, true Fountain of Light and Wisdom, the only creator of all things, to mercifully pour forth into my shadowed understanding the radiance of your love, that it might purge the twofold darkness of sin and ignorance into which I was born.

You, who have given voice to the tongues of infants, instruct my tongue also, and pour forth the grace of your blessing onto my lips.

Grant me prompt understanding, sure memory, direct and easy comprehension, insightful interpretation, and graciousness in speaking.

Launch, O Jesus, my beginning, guide my progress, and let my end be only yourself, who are true God and true Man, living and reigning through all the ages of ages. Amen.

Everything Eternal

Oversee, O my God, my life, that I might do what you ask of me; allow me to see and permit me to do whatever is fitting and profitable to my soul.

Lead me not, O Lord my God, into excessive wealth or want, lest I put my trust in riches, or despair in misery.

Let me take no joy or sorrow, save in what would lead me to you or from you. Let me delight only in pleasing you and fear only displeasing you.

O Lord, let all passing things seem worthless to me and let everything eternal become my treasure. May I despise any joy apart from you and seek nothing that is without you. Make carrying burdens for you my relaxation, O Lord, and rest without you itself a burden.

The Holy Cross

Cross, my certain salvation,
Cross, whom I ever adore,
Cross of the Lord, be with me,
Cross, my refuge, forever more.

St. Thomas More

1478–1535

Immortalized as "a man for all seasons," St. Thomas More was lord chancellor of England under King Henry VIII. He was also a husband, father, lawyer, businessman, politician, and author.

St. Thomas would have been better known to historians than to hagiographers had not his conscience disallowed him to support Henry's divorce from Catherine of Aragon and subsequent marriage to Anne Boleyn. Thomas carefully danced around the issue until Henry demanded an oath of support that declared Catherine's daughter, Mary, to be illegitimate and made Anne's daughter the heir apparent. That was the one thing Thomas could not do. For his refusal he was imprisoned for more than a year in the Tower of London before finally being beheaded.

At his death he announced, "I die the King's good servant, but God's first."

On Behalf of an Enemy

Almighty God, have mercy on [Name]
and on all that bear me evil will, and would do me harm,
and on their faults and mine together.
By such easy, tender, merciful means as your own infinite wisdom can best devise;
vouchsafe to amend and redress and make us saved souls in heaven together,
where we may ever live and love together with you and your blessed saints.

A Godly Meditation

(Written in the Tower of London a year before he was beheaded)

Give me your grace, good Lord, to set the world at nought,
to set my mind fast upon you and not to hang upon the blast of men's mouths.
To be content to be solitary.
Not to long for worldly company,
little and little utterly to cast off the world, and rid my mind of the business thereof.
Not to long to hear of any worldly things,

but that the hearing of worldly fantasies may be to
  me displeasant.
Gladly to be thinking of God,
busily to labor to love him.
To know my own vility and wretchedness,
to humble and meeken myself under the mighty
  hand of God,
to bewail my sins passed;
for the purging of them, patiently to suffer adversity.
Gladly to bear my purgatory here,
to be joyful of tribulations,
to walk the narrow way that leads to life.
To bear the cross with Christ,
to have the last thing—death—in remembrance,
to have ever before my eye death, that is ever at
  hand;
to make death no stranger to me;
to foresee and consider the everlasting fire of hell;
to pray for pardon before the Judge comes.
To have continually in mind the passion that
  Christ suffered for me;
for his benefits incessantly to give him thanks,
to buy the time again that I before have lost.
To abstain from vain confabulations,
to eschew light foolish mirth and gladness;
to cut off unnecessary recreations.
Of worldly substance, friends, liberty, life and all—
to set the loss at nought for the winning of Christ.

To think my worst enemies my best friends,
for the brethren of Joseph could never have done
him so much good
with their love and favor as they did him with
their malice and hatred.

St. Titus Brandsma

1881–1942

If St. Titus had kept his mouth shut, he might not have become a saint! But silence is not the path to sanctity. An author, journalist, and national spiritual adviser to the Dutch Catholic journalists, Titus first spoke out against Hitler's Nürnberg Laws, which prohibited marriage or sexual relations between Jews and Germans. He sealed his fate when he mandated to the Dutch Catholic press that it was not possible for them to print Nazi propaganda and remain Catholic. That proclamation put him on the Nazis' most-wanted list as "that dangerous little friar." The journey to Dachau had begun.

Because of his frail health, St. Titus lasted only five weeks in the infamous prison camp. The nurse who treated him at the camp "hospital" gave an account of his last days. Even as he lay dying, he tried to bring her back to her Catholic faith. He gave her his rosary over her protests that she had forgotten the prayers. "Well," he said, "if you can't say the first part, surely you can still say, 'Pray for us sinners.'" She administered a fatal injection to him on July 26, 1942.

The story doesn't end there. The nurse was so impressed by Titus that she returned to her faith after the war and eventually came forward to testify to his cause for sainthood.

Prayer in Dachau

Dear Lord, when looking up to you, I see your loving eyes on me;
Love overflows my humble heart, knowing what faithful friend you art.
A cup of sorrow I foresee, which I accept for love of you.
The painful way I wish to go;
The only way to God I know.
My soul is full of peace of light;
Although in pain, this light shines bright.
For here you keep to your breast
My longing heart to find there rest.

Leave me here freely alone,
In cell where never sunlight shown.
Should no one ever speak to me,
This golden silence makes me free!
For though alone, I have no fear;
Never were you, O Lord, so near.
Sweet Jesus, please, abide with me;
My deepest peace I find in you.

St. Vincent Ferrer

c. 1350–1419

If power walkers need a patron, St. Vincent Ferrer is their man. In his evangelistic zeal, he walked across Europe four times. St. Vincent earned his greatest fame as a Dominican preacher, although he also performed miracles and advised the pope and secular rulers.

Once, Vincent got caught in the middle of the Avignon popes. The Council of Constance asked the two rival popes to abdicate so that a new, legitimate pope could be elected. The Roman pope agreed, but St. Vincent's friend Benedict XIII refused. That put Vincent in the unhappy position of having to advise the faithful to withdraw their support from Benedict.

While his preaching inspired thousands, he got one point wrong: he thought that the Second Coming would occur in his lifetime. Nevertheless, his legacy is one of repentance and deep personal commitment to the Lord. The first prayer below is part of a longer one asking for a happy and holy death.

For a Happy Death

O Lord, since many different dangers and temptations may occur, should it happen (God forbid) that through them I deviate from that Holy Faith, either at the time of death or some other confusion of mind, or should I consent to any sin, I make profession of it here and now before your Most Holy Majesty, and in the presence of your most glorious mother Mary, my Guardian Angel, my Holy Father Dominic, and all the saints.

For Mercy

Have mercy on me, O Lord, for I have cried to you all the day. Give joy to the soul of your servant, for to you, O Lord, I have lifted up my soul. Have mercy on us, O Lord, have mercy on us, for we are greatly filled with contempt. Glory be to the Father, and to the Son, and to the Holy Spirit. As it was in the beginning, is now, and ever shall be, world without end. Amen.

St. Vincent Pallotti

1795–1850

St. Vincent Pallotti, the son of a Roman grocer, devoted his entire life to helping ordinary people grow in holiness. No ivory-towered theology for him! Once, he wrote to a professor, "You are not cut out for the silence and austerities of Trappists and hermits. Be holy in the world, in your social relationships, in your work and your leisure, in your teaching duties and your contacts with publicans and sinners." Following his own advice, he organized schools for shoemakers, joiners, gardeners, tailors, coachmen, and young workers, saying, "Holiness is simply to do God's will, always and everywhere."

Like St. Philip Neri before him, Vincent Pallotti would do almost anything to help reconcile sinners to God. Once, he dressed up like an old woman to reach the side of a dying man who swore he would shoot the first priest who came near.

Of him it was said, "He did all that he could; as for what he couldn't do—well, he did that too."

Prayer at Death

Not the intellect, but God;
not the will, but God;
not the soul, but God;
not taste, but God;
not touch, but God;
not the heart, but God;
not the body, but God;
not food and drink, but God;
not clothing, but God;
not repose in bed, but God;
not riches, but God;
not distinctions, but God; . . .
God in all and always.
Jesus, bless the congregation: a blessing of goodness, a blessing of wisdom. . . .

(He died before he was able to finish the final line: "a blessing of power.")

William of Saint-Thierry

1085–1148

One of many saints who entered religious life at an early age, lived abstentiously, and died without fanfare, William of Saint-Thierry is most remembered for being a good friend of St. Bernard of Clairvaux. William spent much of his life as the abbot of St. Nicaise in Reims. His primary concern was theology, being the first to discuss serious errors in the works of Peter Abelard. He also wrote biblical commentaries and a life of St. Bernard.

For Forgiveness

Pardon us, O Lord, pardon us.
We beg to shift the blame for our sins,
We make excuses.
But no one can hide from the light of your truth,
which both enlightens those who turn to it,
And exposes those who turn away.

Even our blood and our bones are visible to you,
Who created us out of dust.
How foolish we are to think that we can rule our own lives,
Satisfying our own desires, without thought of you.
How stupid we are to imagine that we can keep our sins hidden.
But although we may deceive other people,
We cannot deceive you, and since you see into our hearts,
We cannot deceive ourselves,
For your light reveals to us our own spiritual corruption.
Let us, therefore, fall down before you, weeping with tears of shame.
May your judgement give new shape to our souls.
May your power mold our hearts to reflect your love.
May your grace infuse our minds, so that our thoughts reflect your will.

St. Zechariah

first century

Zechariah is one of those biblical characters who get short shrift. Not only is he overshadowed by his wife, but he is often overlooked in the story of his son.

Zechariah was the husband of Elizabeth—the cousin of the Blessed Virgin—and the father of John the Baptist. Talk about being caught in the middle! Although he realized his son would be a prophet, one wonders if he recognized that John would be the last of the "holy prophets from of old."

Zechariah's prayer, which Scripture says resulted when he was filled with the Holy Spirit, is one of the New Testament's most beautiful songs of praise, standing as it does between the psalms of the Old Testament and the promises of the New Testament.

Song of Zechariah

Blessed be the Lord, the God of Israel,
for he has visited and brought redemption to his people.
He has raised up a horn for our salvation
within the house of David his servant,
even as he promised through the mouth of his holy prophets from of old:
salvation from our enemies and from the hand
of all who hate us,
to show mercy to our fathers
and to be mindful of his holy covenant
and of the oath he swore to Abraham our father,
and to grant us that,
rescued from the hand of enemies,
without fear we might worship him
in holiness and righteousness
before him all our days.
And you, child, will be called prophet of the Most High,
for you will go before the Lord to prepare his ways,
to give his people knowledge of salvation
through the forgiveness of their sins,
because of the tender mercy of our God
by which the daybreak from on high will visit us

to shine on those who sit in darkness and death's
shadow,
to guide our feet into the path of peace.

Acknowledgments continued from copyright page

St. Dimitrii of Rostov, "Come, My Light," p. 68, excerpted from *The Orthodox Way*, by Bishop Kallistos Ware, copyright © 1979 by St. Vladimir's Seminary Press. Used by permission of St. Vladimir's Seminary Press, 575 Scarsdale Road, Crestwood, NY 10707.

St. Francis of Assisi, "God's Greatness," pp. 95–96, excerpted from *St. Francis of Assisi: Omnibus of Sources*, translated by Benen Fahy, copyright © 1991 by Franciscan Press. Used by permission of Franciscan Press.

St. Gertrude the Great, "Union with God," p. 104, excerpted from *Gertrude of Helfta,* translated by Margaret Winkworth, copyright © 1993 by Paulist Press. Used by permission of Paulist Press, www.paulistpress.com.

St. Hildegard of Bingen, "The Branch," p. 113, excerpted from "Antiphon 8," by Barbara Grant, from *Medieval Women's Visionary Literature*, edited by Elizabeth Petroff, copyright © 1986 by Oxford University Press, Inc. Used by permission of Oxford University Press, Inc.

St. John (Don) Bosco, "Prayer in Illness," p. 127, excerpted from *Don Bosco: A Spiritual Portrait,* by Edna Beyer Phelan, copyright © 1963 by Doubleday & Company. Used by permission of Doubleday, a division of Random House, Inc.

Blessed Mary of Jesus Crucified, "For Ever and Always" and "Take My Soul," pp. 177–78, excerpted from *Mariam the Little Arab*, by Amédée Brunot, S.C.J., translated by Sister Miriam of Jesus, O.S.B. Used by permission of Sister Miriam of Jesus.

St. Maximilian Kolbe, "God's Eternal Love," pp. 180–81, excerpted from *Stronger Than Hatred: A Collection of Spiritual Writings*, copyright © 1988 by New City Press. Used by permission of New City Press.

St. Symeon the New Theologian, "God's Majesty," pp. 217–18, excerpted from *Hymns of Divine Love,* by St. Symeon the New Theologian, translated by George A. Maloney, S.J., copyright © 1978 by Dimension Books, Inc. Used by permission of Dimension Books, Inc.

All attempts were made to contact the original copyright owners of the following works. If you hold the copyright to any of the works below, please contact Woodeene Koenig–Bricker so that proper acknowledgment may be made in future editions.

St. Alphonsus Liguori, "To the Holy Spirit," "For Five Graces," and "Morning Offering," pp. 6–8, excerpted from *Traditional Catholic Prayers,* compiled and edited by Msgr. Charles J. Dollen, Our Sunday Visitor.

St. Anselm, "For Understanding," pp. 13–14, excerpted from *Traditional Catholic Prayers,* compiled and edited by Msgr. Charles J. Dollen, Our Sunday Visitor.

St. Benedict of Nursia, "Benedict's Pledge," pp. 25–27, excerpted from *Traditional Catholic Prayers,* compiled and edited by Msgr. Charles J. Dollen, Our Sunday Visitor.

St. Bernard of Clairvaux, "The Heart of Jesus," p. 33, excerpted from *Traditional Catholic Prayers,* compiled and edited by Msgr. Charles J. Dollen, Our Sunday Visitor.

St. Catherine of Siena, "Thanksgiving," p. 54, excerpted from *Traditional Catholic Prayers,* compiled and edited by Msgr. Charles J. Dollen, Our Sunday Visitor.

St. Clare, "Hymn of Praise," pp. 60–61, excerpted from *Traditional Catholic Prayers,* compiled and edited by Msgr. Charles J. Dollen, Our Sunday Visitor.

St. Elizabeth Ann Seton, "Deliver Me from Evil," p. 77, excerpted from *Elizabeth Seton: An American Woman,* by Leonard Feeney, Our Sunday Visitor, 1975.

St. Ignatius of Loyola, "A Servant Prayer," pp. 118–19, excerpted from *Traditional Catholic Prayers,* compiled and edited by Msgr. Charles J. Dollen, Our Sunday Visitor.

St. Margaret Mary Alacoque, "Sacred Heart," p. 162, excerpted from *Traditional Catholic Prayers,* compiled and edited by Msgr. Charles J. Dollen, Our Sunday Visitor.

St. Mary Magdalen De' Pazzi, "All Treasures," p. 175, excerpted from *Traditional Catholic Prayers,* compiled and edited by Msgr. Charles J. Dollen, Our Sunday Visitor.

Thomas À Kempis, "My Hope and My Crown," pp. 234–35, excerpted from *Traditional Catholic Prayers,* compiled and edited by Msgr. Charles J. Dollen, Our Sunday Visitor.

St. Thomas More, "On Behalf of an Enemy" and "A Godly Meditation," pp. 242–44, excerpted from *Traditional Catholic Prayers,* compiled and edited by Msgr. Charles J. Dollen, Our Sunday Visitor.